HAUNTED AMERICA

Vol. 1

Stories of Ghosts, Hauntings and the Unexplained

G.W.

Mullins

LOTM
PUBLISHING

Light Of The Moon Publishing

ISBN: 978-1-958221-27-3

First Printing

This is a work of fiction. Names, characters, businesses, places, events, and incidents are either the products of the author's imagination or used in a fictitious manner. Any resemblance to actual persons, living or dead, or actual events is purely coincidental.

Light Of The Moon Publishing has allowed this work to remain exactly as the author intended, verbatim, without editorial input.

Printed in the United States of America

For further information, on his writing, visit G.W. Mullins' website at http://gwmullins.wix.com/books

For books available from G.W. Mullins in Hardback,
Paperback and eBook

Visit: https://gwmullins.wixsite.com/books

Or scan the QR Code below

Links to G.W. Mullins pages are on Linktree
https://linktr.ee/gw.mullins

Rise Of The Snow Queen Series

What begins as a simple, bittersweet tale about a man turned into a polar bear, grandly unfolds into a rich, mythical adventure in this best-selling book series.

Based on Hans Christian Andersen's fairy tale, author G.W. Mullins expands on this story creating a new mythology that takes readers into the world of snow and ice.

Long before the adventures of Gerda and Kai, this story takes readers to a remote mountain village, where Winter claims lives, at the Snow Queen's command. The story goes back to the Mirror and how it cracked, sending its shards into the world to infect the innocent.

This reimagining embarks on a much more adult tone with the mood turning rather sinister, as the Snow Queen battles to obtain the mirror. The story will capture and pull you in as Gerda and Kai make their appearances by the third book in the series.

Rise Of The Snow Queen Series

Book One: The Polar Bear King

Book Two: The War Of The Witches

Book Three: The Story Of Gerda And Kai

From the Dead Of Night Series

Death Is Only The Beginning. Daniel walked into the land of the dead. Now the dead want him back!

Daniel Stratton died in a tragic accident. His life should have been over, but it was not. His spirit spent the next sixty years trying to communicate with the people who came to the cemetery. Then, Jen came one night to the mausoleum, seeking refuge from a life that was spinning out of control. It was there she found Daniel.

As they work to free him from the cemetery; they learn that the Light comes for all dead, Daniel is forced to enter it. Inside he sees seven Shadow People within the light, and each one marks him. Daniel knows these Shadows will come for him. Each one in the body of human who has just died. To survive, Daniel and Jen must escape the "Shadows" that are coming for them.

From the Dead Of Night Series

Book One: Daniel Is Waiting

Book Two: Daniel Returns

Book Three Daniel Awakens

Book Four: Daniel's Fate

Messages From The Other Side Series

Best-selling author G.W. Mullins shares his personal journey toward understanding death, the afterlife, and communication with spirits of loved ones who have passed over. In "Messages From The Other Side Stories of the Dead, Their Communication, and Unfinished Business," Mullins tells of dealing with the grief of his mother's passing and the reassurance of an after-death communication that totally changed his outlook towards death and grief.

This book not only tells of Mullins' personal journey into understanding but also guides others to understand why we receive communications and the signs to look for. Mullins also explores visitation dreams and tells of his own personal experience in the area and shares the stories of others who have had similar experiences.

This book highlights the author's personal journey in an exploration for knowledge, and his understanding that, without question, there is life after death.

Messages From The Other Side Series

Book One: Messages From The Other Side

Book Two: Crossing Over

Rise Of The Dark Lighter Series

Mullins returns to the familiar world he created for the "From The Dead Of Night" series while building a new story in this universe. In the book "Daniel's Fate," Mullins left his audience with an ending that promised more. In this latest book, he delivers with a continuation of the final battle between good and evil.

In order to save his uncle, Malachi is forced to summon Santa Muerte, the deity of death. He offers a year of his life in exchange for her help. With his soul on the line, he must do her bidding, to regain his freedom.

The dead begin to rise, as Angels and Demons prepare to wage war for control of humanity. Malachi must choose a side as Armageddon begins.

"Dark Awakening" is the first of three books from "Rise Of The Dark Lighter." This new series is a continuation of his "From The Dead Of Night" books.

Rise Of The DarkLighter

Book One: Dark Awakening

Book Two: Night Of The Demon

Vengeance
A Paranormal Murder Mystery

"Mystery, Murder, Paranormal Events, and a story that leaves you guessing as the bodies stack up."
– Matthew Trent OutLoud Magazine

After the death of her father, Danni starts a new life in a seaside town in New York where she and her mother move into a strange Gothic house with a terrible history. From the moment Danni gets there, she feels she is being watched. She is sure they are not alone in the house.

As Danni learns of her new home, she is told of a past resident who fell to her death on the nearby cliffs at the same time that her teenage daughter, Elizabeth, disappeared.

Elizabeth's spirit appears to Danni and claims that her mother's death was a murder, not suicide, and asks for Danni's help in bringing the dangerous killer to justice.

The mystery unfolds as Danni enlists the help of the hunky new friend she has made named Joe. A romance develops between them, but does Joe know more about the murder and disappearance than he is letting on? Will Danni live to solve the murder?

Dream Walker Series

They say a dream is a wish, but what they forgot to mention, nightmares are dreams too. As the city darkens and humans descend into sleep, a powerful being enters the Earth Realm. This mysterious creature, known as the Sandman, takes control of our dreams and battles for control of souls.

After a boy named Zach is taken into the other realm, he awakens to a new world filled with nightmares. He is joined by two others, Daniel and Jen, as they battle to escape the Dream World and find their way back to reality. Beware the Sandman is coming.

"Enter The Sandman" is the first of three books from Author G.W. Mullins' "Dream Walker" book series. This new series, shares a couple of familiar faces from the Best-Selling "From The Dead Of Night" books, featuring the Best-Selling titles "Daniel Is Waiting" and "Daniel Returns."

Dream Walker Series

Book One: Enter The SandMan

Book Two: Wide Awake In Dreamland

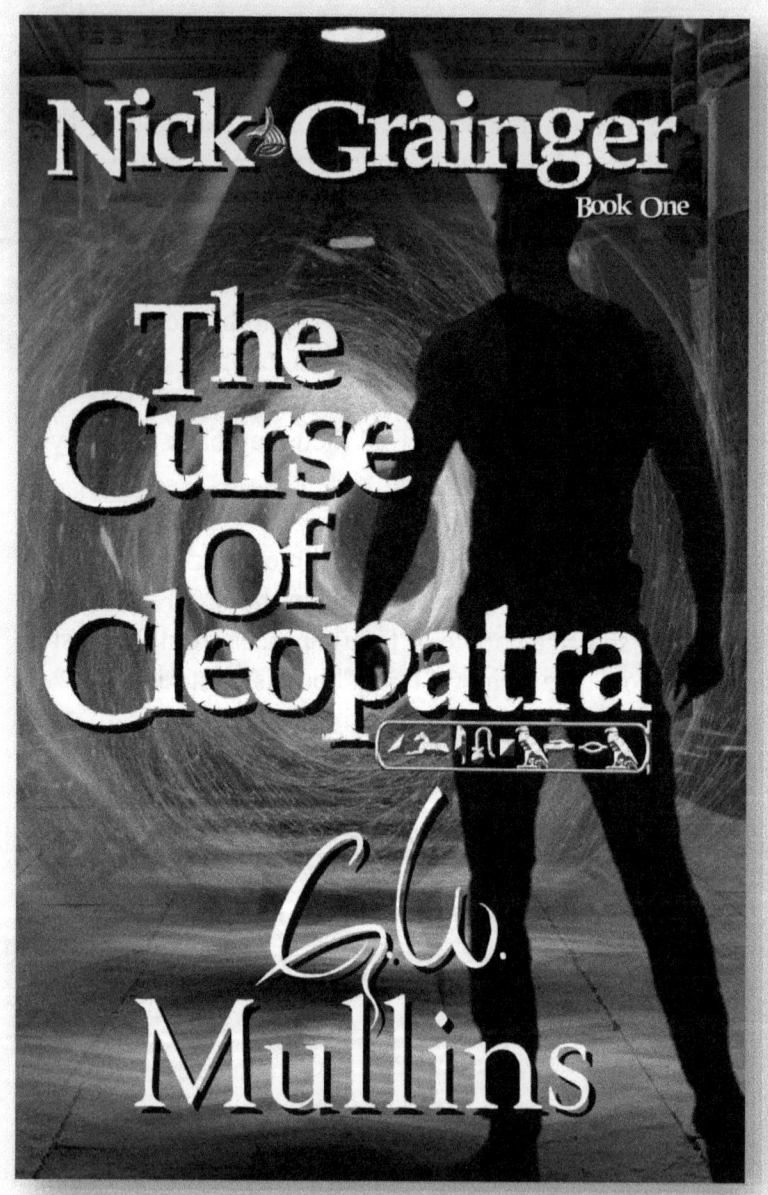

Nick Grainger Series

Building on the concept that the Earth was once populated by a superior Ancient Alien race, this new book series takes the reader on an adventure through gateways to the multiverse.

Nick Grainger, a young college student working on an archaeological dig in Egypt, accidentally activates a gate to a different universe. He along with three of his companions, are thrown into the ancient alien gateway system between parallel worlds. Lost in the multiverse, they must search for a way home.

On their journey, their gate opens into strange new worlds, similar to their Earth, but in different times and in places. It is on one such Earth, they arrive in Egypt, not as it was in the days of the ancients. Now, it is a place where a technologically advanced race of gods rule.

These new gods of Egypt live through taking the bodies of human hosts. It is there, Nick must fight his ultimate battle, as he is designated to be host to the god Anubis.

"Nick Grainger The Curse Of Cleopatra" is the first of three books from Author G.W. Mullins' "Nick Grainger" book series.

FROM THE AUTHOR OF "RISE OF THE SNOW QUEEN - THE POLAR BEAR
KING" AND "DANIEL IS WAITING"

THE LEGEND OF
WHITE
BEAR

Extended Edition

EVERYONE HAS A
BEAST WITHIN THEM.

G.W.
MULLINS

The Legend Of White Bear (Extended Edition)

Nita's tribe faced the coming of the bear every full moon. When it came, many would die.

To protect his daughter, the chief sent her away to live in a rip in time and space, called the void. He told her it was for her protection, but he never told her of the bear's history.

One member of his tribe was burdened with carrying the bear shapeshifter trait. For a lifetime, they would be cursed with being both human and bear until their death. Then a new child would be born to carry the trait.

While in the void, Nita discovers the true horrifying history of the white bear.

The Convergence Series

In the year 2029, the third world war will begin. After the global population is pushed to the brink of insanity from the recent pandemic, they plunge into hatred and violence. With the space race to colonize the moon, man seeks a refuge from the insanity, and the impending environmental destruction brought on by decades of pollution.

In the worldwide confusion, the inevitable happens, when a single nuclear warhead is fired by the command of an insane dictator. Nuclear retaliations are sent forward, ending in a destruction of the Earth's moon. The end of mankind as we know will begin. Human civilization is cast in ruin. A strange new world rises from the old; a world of mutation, super science, and magic. Witness the Convergence. The countdown begins now.

The Convergence Series

Book Zero: Mass Destruction
Book One: Armageddon

Other titles available from G.W. Mullins include:

Timeless - An Adult Paranormal Romance Novel

Aliens, Gods, And Other Paranormal Native American
Tales

The Native American Story Book Volume 1-5- Stories Of
The American Indians For Children

Walking With Spirits Volumes 1-6 Native American
Myths, Legends, And Folklore

The Native American Cookbook

Star People, Sky Gods, And Other Tales of The Native
American Indians

More Star People, Sky Gods, and Other Paranormal Tales
Of The Native American Indians

For Clarence

Life is wasted on the living.
~ ***Anonymous***

Table Of Contents

Introduction

Whether it's an old house, a forgotten graveyard, a historic hotel…it is the supernatural or the unknown aspect, that can accurately summarize a place that fascinates and horrifies at the same time. Many people who have visited such places describe feelings of uneasiness, hearing unexplained noises, feeling cold spots, and even seeing the dead. Some people have even reported being touched or having their bodies scratched by something menacing.

The questions of life after death have never been fully answered, and this adds to the mystery of these places. There's an eerie feeling about haunted places like they are a connection to a different plane. A place from which others can still communicate with us, and sometimes come back from.

Some people look at these as places of great fascination, a glimpse into the unknown, and a chance to experience something truly unique and incredible. For others, it's a place of terror, that unleashes their fear. No matter which way you look at it, the afterlife is one of the greatest mysteries known to man.

In this book, we will explore these otherworldly locations where the dead still haunt. We will look at the restless spirits that still lurk in these fear-inducing locations. We will walk with the dead.

Haunted America

CHAPTER ONE
SPIRITS, THE DEAD, AND
OTHER THINGS

The majority of people living today believe in ghosts and an afterlife. A poll was taken throughout many different cultures and countries and it was proven, that many of us have indeed had encounters with the unknown and we believe. In the United States alone, one-half of the population supports the idea of the afterlife. That can be supported by the thousands of ghost hunters and investigators in existence.

This widespread pursuit of the paranormal has spread to every corner of every state in the nation. This is no surprise with the recorded number of historical ghostly and unexplained encounters. This all lends to the popularity of the belief in ghosts for centuries.

With the popularity of the paranormal, there has of course been a cross-over into popular media in the forms of books, media, television shows, and more reality-based shows than you can count. This all lends to the consensus that ghosts are real.

In general, ghosts can appear anywhere, but history and perhaps geography, usually provide good reasons why the site may be haunted.

Residual energy hauntings are just locations that "feel" haunted. There may be some activity, and even an apparition or two... but it's the same thing, every time. The activity usually occurs on a certain day or date, and sometimes at a particular time. Or, it might be activated by a specific trigger, such as when a certain song is played on the radio.

Active hauntings are similar to residual energy hauntings, but the ghost (or ghosts) will respond to modern-day events in its vicinity. That is, if you talk to the ghost, it will respond or at least pause what it's doing.

Are you living with ghosts? Most people who've lived in older homes, or stayed in a vintage hotel or inn, have encountered a ghost or two. Whether real or not, the fact is these events do exist and so do paranormal phenomena.

The Most Common Types Of Ghosts And Spirits

1. The Interactive Intelligence

Intelligent ghosts are self-aware and can interact with the living world in a way of communication. They are most often referred to as "interactive hauntings" or "crisis apparitions." By crisis, they often come with a warning to prevent harm or to help the living. Intelligent ghosts can communicate with the living through speech, dreams, writing, or telepathy. History dictates they can move objects, turn on lights, affect electronic devices, and create other physical phenomena.

There are many different theories about why some ghosts are intelligent and others are not. Many experts believe that intelligent ghosts are the spirits of those who died unexpectedly, and who have unfinished business. Others believe that intelligent spirits have a strong emotional attachment to those still living or to something that they loved in life. Still, others believe that these spirits are more evolved and have attained more abilities to reach out to the living.

Regardless of the reason, intelligent spirits can be familiar and unsettling. While they can offer a glimpse into the afterlife, they can also provide a source of comfort or guidance for the living. This is probably why the most common of all ghosts spotted is usually of a deceased person, someone you know, a family member, or perhaps even a historical figure.

One thing to keep in mind is, that there is no scientific evidence to support the existence of ghosts, intelligent or otherwise. While millions of people around the world believe in ghosts and have well-documented cases of alleged paranormal activity, it is up to each individual to choose if they believe or not.

2. Ectoplasm or Ecto-Mist

Have you ever seen a misty fog that appears to be swirling? Depending on the situation, you may have witnessed what paranormal investigators call an ecto-mist.

This mist or vapor can move in a swirling motion or stand still. Many ghost hunters or everyday people have captured these mists on video. Often appearing in white, gray, or black, they have shown themselves to many ghosthunters over the years. Sometimes ecto-mists appear as a way to interact with the living, before becoming a full-bodied apparition. Many people have witnessed them outdoors, in graveyards, battlefields, and historical sites.

Ectoplasm and ecto-mists have been featured in many works of fiction, including movies like Ghostbusters, where it is shown as a green slime that ghosts are made of. However, there is no scientific evidence to support the existence of ectoplasm.

Some paranormal investigators believe that ectoplasm is a real substance that can be detected using specialized equipment. They also claim that ectoplasm can be found in areas where ghosts are present. However, other paranormal investigators are skeptical of the existence of ectoplasm. They argue that the evidence for ectoplasm is often inconclusive.

Whether or not ectoplasm is real, remains a debatable topic. It is a reminder that there is still much we do not know about the nature of ghosts and the afterlife.

3. The Poltergeist

Poltergeist…one of the most recognizable terms used when it comes to the paranormal. The word, German in nature, actually means "Noisy Ghost." It earns its name from the way it reacts to the living, by knocking over things, moving objects, and manipulating the physical environment.

We have all heard the word before, but this is usually the rarest form of haunting. While on the scale of calm to frightening, this is on the more aggressive side of hauntings. The range of appearance can be as simple as knocking on doors, to lights being turned on and off in a room. There have even been occurrences where fires have broken out and been attributed to this type of manifestation.

While we think of ghosts as harmless, this is not always the case with a Poltergeist. While the presence of this entity can be harmless, in some cases, it can intensify. In this case, a living being is unknowingly controlling an extreme amount of energy. Many cases in history have documented this occurrence and, in some cases, turned deadly.

4. Orbs

Orbs are spherical-shaped anomalies that appear in photographs and recorded videos. Many times, ghost hunters capture these spheres in their research of a reportedly haunted location. They are often described as balls of light, but they can also be transparent or have a hazy appearance. While orbs can be any color, they are most commonly seen as white or gold.

Orbs are probably the most photographed type of anomaly. They appear hovering over the ground. Sometimes in the video, they can be seen shooting across the recorded area. It is speculated that orbs are the remains of a soul who died and is traveling among the living.

5. Funnel Ghosts

Funnel Ghosts are often seen as a vortex, which is associated with a cold spot. These are often found in older homes or deserted locations.

When photographed, they appear as a streak of light that blurs out an area of an image. Most times, the light will not show in the initial photography. Then at a later time when images are reviewed, they are very much in view.

Appearing as a wisp of light or a swirling spiral of light, they are often caught in photographs or on video. It is thought these represent the spirit of a deceased loved one who has returned to a location they once knew.

Haunted America

CHAPTER TWO
GHOSTS AT SEA AND BY WATER

Ghosts at sea have been a source of fascination for centuries. There are countless stories of ghostly ships, spectral sailors, and even haunted lighthouses. A death at sea is not only tragic but sudden, with unfinished business or an unsolved mystery, the ghosts of our oceans are cast adrift, lost on the waves of eternity.

From the Flying Dutchman to the Mary Celeste, these tales of the supernatural have captivated the imagination of generations. While ghost ships have their fair share of ghostly tales Lighthouses also have their own ghosts. Most of these stories remind us of the need for closure and the unfairness of death.

Earth's oceans are more dangerous than we give them credit. They have consumed the lives of thousands of sailors, and passengers throughout history. Because of this, there is no shortage of the ghosts produced from the wreckage or the stories they have cast over the waters throughout history.

The Ghost Sailor Of The USS Lexington

For centuries, sailors have been telling tales of supernatural phenomena on the high seas. One of the most haunting and enduring of these stories is that of the ghost sailor of the USS Lexington.

The USS Lexington is an iconic aircraft carrier that has served the United States Navy for many decades. During WWII, this impressive vessel spent 21 months in combat. No fewer than four times, the Japanese reported that the blue ship had sunk, only to find her reappear again. Her nickname became, appropriately, "the Blue Ghost."

While it boasts a rich history of military achievements and bravery, it is also known for something else - its haunted past. Over the years, numerous reports and eerie experiences have fueled the belief that the USS Lexington is a hotbed for paranormal activity.

Today, the ship is a museum known for its historic exhibits and supernatural activity. Over the years many guests have met Charlie, a tour guide who wears a traditional naval uniform. The ship has never actually employed a tour guide named Charlie; the helpful spirit is thought to be the ghost of a sailor.

Charlie is one of the most well-known hauntings on the Lexington, being he was once a young sailor on the ship. Legend has it that Charlie was tragically killed during a fierce battle on the ship. Since then, his spirit has been said to wander the decks, often spotted in the dead of night by bewildered crew members. Many have reported hearing disembodied voices and footsteps, accompanied by an icy chill in the air, which they attribute to Charlie's presence.

As many as 200 visitors to the museum have reported encounters with Charlie. Without exception, the reports indicate the ghostly seaman is a "polite young man" who seems to share a great deal of information about the Lexington's engine room far below deck.

Charlie is not the only ghost to be seen on the ship. Another bone-chilling encounter aboard the USS Lexington is that of a female spirit known as Lady in Blue. According to witnesses, this ghostly apparition roams the narrow corridors of the ship, adorned in a blue dress reminiscent of the naval uniform worn by nurses during World War II. Some claim that she is a nurse who served onboard and lost her life during a tragic incident. Those who have encountered her describe an overwhelming sensation of sadness and despair.

The eerie happenings continue in the engine room of the USS Lexington, where crew members have reported ghostly figures and strange shadows lurking among the machinery. These unexplained phenomena occur even when the space is completely vacant. People have felt an inexplicable sense of anxiety and unease, leading many to believe that the spirits of deceased engine room workers still wander the area, unwilling to let go of their earthly duties.

Other strange occurrences involving a painting and restoration crew on board have been reported. The work crew had taken a break, but when they returned, the work project had mysteriously been finished for them. In other instances, visitors and staff have reported incidents of ship lights going on and off by themselves.

The USS Lexington has a section dedicated to showcasing its haunted history - the Ghosts and Legends tour. No matter if the ghostly history of this ship is true or not, it is clear that the legend of the ghost sailor Charlie of the USS Lexington will live on for many more generations to come.

Ghosts Of The Sheffield Island Lighthouse

The Sheffield Island Lighthouse in Norwalk, Connecticut is a stunning, historic sight to behold. But it is also the site of some spooky sightings that have kept locals and visitors alike talking for decades. It is said that the ghosts of the lighthouse keepers, who lived and worked at the lighthouse, still haunt the area.

Built in 1868 to help ships reach Connecticut's Sheffield Island, this 10-room, Victorian-style lighthouse has a bit of a troubled past.

The Sheffield Island Lighthouse is located off the coast of Norwalk, Connecticut, and is connected to the mainland by a bridge. It was built in 1868 and has been kept in pristine condition ever since. The lighthouse was once home to two families of lighthouse keepers, the Daley family and the Murray family. The families lived and worked at the lighthouse to ensure that ships could safely navigate the treacherous waters near the island.

In 1991, an archaeologist working on historic site preservation reported several mysterious happenings, including mystical music coming from the shores, distant cries for help, and the sound of a foghorn—despite there being no foghorn on the island.

He claimed to hear footsteps in empty rooms, see shadows moving out of the corner of his eye, and feel cold spots. He also said that he would often wake up in the middle of the night to the sound of someone calling his name.

Many believe the sounds of music were the work of the ghost of Captain Robert Sheffield, who originally purchased the islands in the early 1800s (and had a knack for unusual musical instruments).

For over a century, locals and visitors alike have reported strange occurrences at the lighthouse. Some claim to have seen the spectral figures of the former lighthouse keepers wandering the grounds. Others claim to have heard strange noises coming from inside the lighthouse, and some have even reported seeing strange lights in the windows of the lighthouse.

One of the most famous stories about the lighthouse is about a former keeper named Francis Murray. Murray died in 1871, after falling from the lighthouse. Since then, people have reported seeing his ghostly figure at the lighthouse. He is said to be searching for something, although no one knows what.

Another ghost that is said to haunt the lighthouse is that of a former lighthouse keeper named Noah Mosher. Mosher died suddenly in 1872 while watching passing ships with a spyglass. Some people believe that his ghost can still be seen sitting in the lighthouse tower, watching the ships.

The Green Lantern Of St. Martin's Island

At one time, a lighthouse keeper lived on St. Martin's Island, along with his family. His wife passed away and left the man to care for his children alone. He loved his children and wanted them to get the best education. He bought a small shallow-draft boat for the children to row to the mainland to go to school every day.

The children did as their father asked and rowed to the mainland, went to school, and then rowed the boat back to the lighthouse on St. Martin's Island. One spring as the children were rowing back home from school, a sudden squall overturned the rowboat. The squall sent the boat along with the children, to the depths of the water. The children were not found.

From that day forward, the lighthouse keeper would search the shoreline for his children. He would use the light from a green lantern, and search every night without giving up.

Today, if you visit the mainland and peer out at St. Martin's Island on a stormy night, you may catch a glimpse of the green lantern. Some believe the man is still searching for his children lost to the lake, while others believe he is warning others, so they will not share the same fate.

Haunted St. Augustine Lighthouse, FL

St. Augustine, Florida is home to one of the most haunted lighthouses in the United States: the St. Augustine Lighthouse. The haunted lighthouse dates back to the early 1800s. Since then, visitors and staff have reported numerous strange occurrences.

The St. Augustine Lighthouse is visited by nearly 225,000 people annually, but it's just as well-known for its otherworldly visitors. Several tragic events that occurred at the now-historic site have contributed to the alleged paranormal activity.

The first reported sighting of the ghost occurred in 1822, when a sailor claimed to have seen a figure, believed to be an original lighthouse keeper, standing at the top of the lighthouse. Since then, numerous visitors have reported seeing the ghost, often described as a large man wearing a long coat and a wide-brimmed hat.

In addition to sightings of ghosts, visitors to the lighthouse have reported hearing strange noises and experiencing a sense of unease. Some visitors have reported feeling a chill in the air when they enter the lighthouse, while others have reported hearing footsteps and strange thumping noises.

The ghost of a lighthouse keeper who fell to his death while painting the structure has been spotted watching over the grounds. And ever since the horrific death of three young girls, who drowned when the cart they were playing in broke and fell into the ocean, visitors have claimed to hear the sounds of children playing in and around the lighthouse.

The present-day St. Augustine Lighthouse was built in 1874 but it is not the original lighthouse. The original was built in the 1600s, but tidal erosion marked an end to it. The current lighthouse was built by the U.S. Government, which bought parcels of land from several Florida residents, to house the project. A death at the original lighthouse and a dispute from a neighbor during the second build is only the start of the tragedy, that has occurred on this spot, making this one of the most haunted places in America.

There are two possible ghosts attributed to the original lighthouse, Mr. Andreu, the original lighthouse keeper who fell to his death while painting the tower, and Dr. Ballard. Being one of the original landowners, Dr. Ballard, disputed his neighbors over the land deal with the government and reports are that he claimed he would never leave his land. Some say, he never did.

There are also reports from staff and visitors alike of cigar smells throughout the lighthouse. This can be attributed to another keeper, Peter Rasmussen who was said to be not only a strict and meticulous manager but was always seen smoking his favorite cigar.

The lighthouse would undergo a renovation during the late 1800s. The head of that renovation was Hezekiah Pitee. The main obstacle to overcome during this renovation was getting supplies up to the lighthouse. This was overcome by a tram system that ran from the lighthouse down to where the supplies were brought in.

Pitee's daughters Eliza (13), Carrie (4), and Mary (15). along with a friend. were always playing around the lighthouse. It has been reported that the girls would often ride down the tramway for fun. One day in 1873, the girls rode the tramway, but it broke loose, slid down the hill, and into the bay. All of the girls drowned, and it is this tragedy that has produced one of the most well-known ghosts of the St. Augustine Lighthouse.

Staff and visitors have claimed to hear two girls laughing in the tower, along with footsteps running up and down the steps. It is the eldest girl, Mary, that people claim to have seen in several places. She has been seen wearing the same blue velvet dress and blue hair bow, she had on when the accident occurred. Interestingly, the third girl in the accident, an African American has never been seen.

The Keeper's House was built right beside the lighthouse, and there have also been reports of a girl appearing and disappearing in the house. In the 1950's the last keeper refused to stay in the house, because of the sighting, and footsteps heard of the little girl

The most intriguing of all the reports is that of the upstairs door. It is padlocked every night by the closing employee and has motion-sensor lights, as well as a security alarm, at the top of the lighthouse. Employees opening the lighthouse the next morning, have said there are times when the door has been unlocked, and standing open when they go to unlock it the next day.

Ghosts Of The RMS Queen Mary

Aside from a brief stint as a warship in World War II, the RMS Queen Mary served as a luxury ocean liner from 1936 to 1967. During that time, it was the site of at least one murder, a sailor being crushed to death by a door in the engine room, and children drowning in the pool.

This ship was started in 1930 by the Cunard Steamship Company and one year later, stopped due to the depression in the UK. Construction resumed in 1934 and in that same year, Cunard Steamship Company merged with The White Star Line who would coincidentally own and operate the Titanic. The ship saw its maiden voyage in May of 1936.

She was built for transatlantic civilian service but that would not be its legacy. In 1940 she was painted grey and given an ominous new name, Gray Ghost. Its new service for World War II would be to transport up to 15,000 troops at a time, mainly for the United States War effort.

The city of Long Beach purchased the ship in 1967 and turned it into a hotel, and it still serves that purpose today—although the reported ghosts of the deceased passengers get to stay for free.

It is said that the ghosts of the Queen Mary still wander its hallways and decks. One of the most famous is the ghost of John Pedder, a young stoker who was crushed to death in the engine room in 1966. His ghost has been seen by many witnesses, often in the same spot where he died. He dressed in blue coveralls and sporting a beard walked down the corridor and disappeared where the old door 13 used to be.

Other reported ghosts include a woman in a white dress who was believed to have been a passenger on board the ship in the 1930s, a little girl named Jackie, who drowned in the pool during one of the ship cruises, is said to haunt the swimming pool area, and a young boy who is often seen running around the decks.

The stories of the ghosts of the Queen Mary have made it one of the most famous haunted places in the world. Several ghost tours are offered to visitors, allowing them to explore the ship and learn more about its haunted history.

Some of the most famous ghosts that are said to haunt the Queen Mary include:

The Lady in White: This ghost is often seen wandering the ship's decks, wearing a long white dress. She is said to be the spirit of a bride who died on the ship during her honeymoon.

The Engineer: This ghost is often seen in the ship's engine room. He is said to be the spirit of an engineer who was killed in an accident in the engine room.

The Children: These ghosts are often seen playing in the ship's third-class swimming pool. They are said to be the spirits of children who drowned in the pool.

In addition to these famous ghosts, many other ghosts are said to haunt the Queen Mary. These ghosts include the ghosts of passengers, crew members, and other people who have died on the ship or in its vicinity.

Seguin Island Lighthouse

In the northeastern corner of the U.S., sitting high on its barren island made of rock is the Sequin Island Lighthouse. This lighthouse, located at the mouth of the Kennebec River in Georgetown, Maine, is the second lighthouse that was ever built in the States. It is also one of the oldest in the U.S. The rock island is located in an area that is frequently shrouded in fog.

The history of Seguin Island Light Station is filled with strange and tragic stories.

One is that of the first light keeper, who died penniless and boatless on the island. Some say his ghost has haunted the keepers that came after him. There have been sightings of a ghost who has been named the "Old Captain". Usually seen climbing the staircase of the tower as if heading upstairs to tend to the light.

One night the old furnishings were being removed from the premises. The man in charge of the crew moving the furniture was awakened in the middle of the night, by the "Old Captain" who asked him not to take the furniture, and to leave his home alone. The man didn't grant the request, and the next day after the furniture had been loaded onto a boat to be lowered into the water. The cable mysteriously snapped. The boat and everything in it fell onto the rocks below and were destroyed. Perhaps, the "Old Captain" got his way after all.

Another frequent sighting is that of a young girl running up and down the stairs, waving to those who see her. She has been heard laughing, and bouncing a ball in a room upstairs. History shows that a young girl died on the island and was buried near the lighthouse.

Perhaps the most tragic incident that occurred on the island is that of a former caretaker in the mid-1800s who was driven insane and murdered his wife. He then took his own life. It is said the caretaker brought his wife to live with him at the lighthouse shortly after they were married. As time went by, she became depressed and sullen. Then, he bought her a piano, to help cheer her up.

Unfortunately, she didn't memorize the songs she knew and had to play from sheet music. Since she had only had one piece of sheet music on the island, she played the same song over and over. Then one day her husband finally took an axe to the piano and her. He then killed himself. Passing ships have reported they can hear the faint sound of a piano floating out over the waves on quiet evenings.

Seguin Island is also said to be haunted by a mysterious ghost known as the "Gray Lady." According to local legend, the Gray Lady is the spirit of a woman who died in a tragic accident on the island.

The Gray Lady is said to haunt the lighthouse and the surrounding area. She has been seen by visitors and lighthouse keepers on the island, often seen pacing back and forth in the lightkeeper's quarters. Those who have seen her describe her as wearing a gray dress with her hair in a bun, and she has often been seen in the area of the oil house and the fog signal building.

Although no one is certain who the Gray Lady is or why she is haunting the island, some believe she is the spirit of a woman who drowned in one of the island's ponds. Others believe she is the spirit of a woman who died in a fire at the lighthouse.

The Gray Lady is just one of many ghost stories that surround the island. There are tales of a ghost ship, mysterious lights, and a ghostly dog roaming the island.

The North Island Lighthouse

The North Island Lighthouse in Georgetown, South Carolina is rumored to be haunted by the ghosts of a former lightkeeper and his young daughter, Annie.

According to legend, the lightkeeper and Annie lived in the lighthouse for many years. They were very close, and Annie was her father's only companion. One day, a storm hit the coast, and the lighthouse was damaged. The lightkeeper was injured, and Annie was trapped in the lighthouse. She tried to help her father, but she was unable to free him. The lightkeeper died from his injuries, and Annie was left alone in the lighthouse.

Annie eventually died in there, and her ghost is said to haunt it to this day. She is often seen standing in the window, looking out at the sea. Some people believe that Annie's ghost is protecting the lighthouse and the ships that pass by.

Another ghost story associated with the North Island Lighthouse is the story of the "Lady in White." She is said to be the ghost of a woman who drowned near the lighthouse. She is often seen walking along the beach, wearing a long white dress. Some people believe that the

Lady in White is trying to warn people of the dangers of the sea.

Garrity's Screaming Wife

Old Presque Isle Lighthouse in Michigan is believed to be haunted by a former lighthouse keeper's wife.

Mr. Patrick Garrity was the very last lighthouse keeper at the Presque Isle site and had been appointed to the position by no other than President Lincoln.

It is suggested that the isolation of living in the lighthouse drove Garrity's wife insane, and to prevent her madness from taking over their lives, he kept her locked away.

On windy nights many reports have suggested that you can still hear Mrs. Garrity screaming from within the lighthouse itself.

The Ghost Ship Of Captain Sandovate

Off the coast of New Jersey, you may be witness to an eerie ghost ship that haunts the Atlantic Ocean along the coastline.

Captain Sandovate was a notorious pirate who terrorized the seven seas during the 1700s. His ship, the Ghost Ship, was said to appear out of nowhere, striking fear into the hearts of sailors and merchants alike. The Ghost Ship was said to be cursed, with a strange and eerie presence that no one could explain.

The legend of the Ghost Ship began when Captain Sandovate set sail with his crew of ruthless pirates in search of riches. One night, while they were in the middle of the ocean, they saw an eerie white fog rolling in. The fog was so thick that they could not see anything in front of them. As the fog cleared, they saw a large, black ship looming in front of them. It seemed to be made of shadows, and its sails were billowing with an eerie, green light.

The crew of the Ghost Ship was said to be made up of undead sailors, cursed to wander the seas for eternity. The ship was captained by a figure shrouded in darkness, and his crew was said to be made up of ghosts and ghouls. The ship was also said to be cursed with a strange and powerful force, which could control the weather and sea.

The beginning of this tale is one of the horrifying death of Captain Don Sandovate. He along with his crew sailed from Spain to the New World in search of treasure. He did find gold; however, his crew did not wish to share the wealth with the monarch of Spain. They mutinied and turned on their captain. How they imprisoned the captain was one of the most brutal on record. He was tied to the main mast. He was not allowed food or water. The summer sun was beating down on his body day after day as the sailors turned to piracy.

After many days tied to the mast, Don Sandovate begged for just a sip of water. The men thought this was very amusing and taunted the captain even more by holding water just out of his reach. The captain did not last. He died within a few days after the mutiny. The new captain left his body tied to the mast and plundered his way up the coast. The people of Providence were watching in fear as these heartless men left destruction on their path.

A storm arose on the seas and the ship sank with everyone on board with Captain Sandovate still tied to the mast.

Today, many have seen the ghost ship with its mast broken, the captain's body tied to the main mast, and skeletons as crew members. The skeletons beg ships passing by for a mere sip of water.

Many tales were told about the Ghost Ship of Captain Sandovate, but no one knew what became of it. Some say it still sails the seas, while others believe it has been lost to the depths of the ocean. Whatever the truth may be, the legacy of the Ghost Ship still lives on in the tales of the sea.

The story of the Ghost Ship of Captain Sandovate is a chilling reminder of the dangers of the seas. It is a reminder that even in the face of the unknown, there is still a spark of courage that can keep us going.

Race Rock Lighthouse

When it comes to the ghostly tales of the North East coast, one of the most famous stories is that of the Race Rock Lighthouse, located in New London, Connecticut. The lighthouse was built in 1879 to protect ships from the treacherous rocks of Race Point. It stands at the entrance of Long Island Sound and has a long and sordid history of hauntings.

Race Rock is a series of dangerous rock formations found a few miles offshore. The rocks cause a hazardous flow of ocean currents that collide from two directions at once. When the weather turns for the worst, the waves can become quite high, crashing anything in their path down upon the reef of Race Rock.

From 1829 to 1837, 8 vessels were destroyed upon the dangerous Race Rock reef. This resulted in Congress allocating $3,000 for the construction of a much-needed lighthouse upon the rocky formation in 1838.

Unfortunately, nothing ever came of the proposed foundation, and no lighthouse was built. Instead, buoys and spindles were attempted, but these were terribly unstable and failed miserably.

The government tried again to appropriate funds for a day-beacon, and again for a lighthouse in the 1850's, but most of the money was spent on surveys. Finally, in 1870, congress concluded that it would need at least $150,000 to build a lighthouse structure on such dangerous, unstable terrain. Smith began the design and construction began in 1871, and completed in 1878.

Reports of ghosts and haunting activities began flowing in long before Race Rock Lighthouse was ever erected, attributed to the countless shipwrecks and deaths associated with Race Rock. Numerous Coast Guard employees have reported everything from ghostly apparitions and the sound of footsteps to whispering, yelling, laughter, and disembodied voices calling out their names. Some even claim to have been pushed, touched, and/or poked by these ghosts and refuse to return to the island of Race Rock.

One of the most unusual reports regarding the haunting of Race Rock Lighthouse, told multiple times by different visitors to the island, is that they have heard running water or seen damp footsteps coming from what used to be the location of showers. The showers were removed, and no water ran through the pipes many years ago.

Under the cover of night, ships passing near the Race Rock Lighthouse have continually reported the vision of a shadowy figure in the lighthouse, illuminated as the light passed by. Race Rock Lighthouse is not inhabited by anyone, day or night, as it has been automated for some years now. The only living beings to visit the lighthouse are the Coast Guard maintenance crew, which is intermittent at best, and never during the twilight hours.

While no one seems to know exactly who is haunting the Race Rock Lighthouse, or how many ghostly apparitions may reside there, the lighthouse is certainly quite haunted by ghost activity.

It is said that it is possibly the ghost of the first lightkeeper, Joseph Wilson, who still haunts the lighthouse. According to local legend, Wilson lived in the lighthouse with his family until he died in 1883, and ever since his spirit has been seen wandering the halls of the lighthouse.

The ghost of Wilson is said to linger in the main living quarters of the lighthouse. He can often be seen sitting in a rocking chair, staring out into the sea. He is also said to appear on the highest level of the lighthouse, where he can be heard humming softly and walking back and forth.

Another ghostly presence is said to haunt the lighthouse: the spirit of a young girl. Legend has it that she was the daughter of one of the keepers and went missing in the lighthouse one night. Her spirit is said to wander the halls of the lighthouse, searching for her missing father.

The most famous ghost of Race Rock Lighthouse is that of the mysterious white lady. She is said to appear on the balcony of the lighthouse, dressed in a long white gown. She is often seen staring out into the sea, searching for a loved one who never returned from their voyage.

Whether or not these stories are true, they have certainly made Race Rock Lighthouse one of the most famous haunted locations in the North East.

Point Lookout Lighthouse

Point Lookout Lighthouse is a historic landmark on the coast of Maryland. The lighthouse is situated within Point Lookout State Park but is no longer operational. According to local folklore, the ghosts of Point Lookout Lighthouse remain quite active in their duties.

Erected in 1830 by draftsman John Donahoo, the Point Lookout Lighthouse was commissioned five years prior when the federal government deemed it necessary to establish an illumining warning to sailors of the shoals at the mouth of the Potomac River.

The Point Lookout Lighthouse is unique in the sense that it was created in the fashion of a traditional house, rather than the standard lighthouse of cylindrical, elevated design. The circular edifice that encases the light itself is the same, but below this point is a story and a half of customary dwelling. The lighthouse debuted its beam on September 20, 1830.

In 1883, an additional story was built onto the Point Lookout Lighthouse to enable two employees and their families to reside within the home, thereby sharing the duties of the lighthouse.

The haunting of Point Lookout Lighthouse goes well beyond the lighthouse itself as the entire state park has its ghostly legends, dating back through the Civil War. This rolled over to the lighthouse as well, as Confederate soldiers clashed with the Union army, and prisoners were held hostage within the lighthouse.

This explains the mass of EVP recordings collected by paranormal investigators over the last decades. More than two dozen individual, disembodied voices have been caught on tape, including male and female voices.

Point Lookout Lighthouse is haunted by several spectral ghosts as well, including that of Ann Davis, the wife of the original keeper of the lighthouse. Reports of her ghosts manifesting at the top of the stairs have come in on numerous occasions, often wearing a long blue skirt and white blouse.

Photographic evidence of paranormal activity at Point Lookout Lighthouse has been captured, but none so famous as "The Ghost of Point Lookout", a prominent photo taken in the late 1970s during a séance.

The photo depicted former lighthouse resident Laura Berg grasping a candle in her hand in the center of the picture, while an apparition of a soldier sat idly in the corner of the room. He was dressed in full combat gear and weapon. He had one leg comfortably crossed over the other as he leaned against the wall. No one present at the séance noticed the gentleman at the time, but the picture indubitably revealed his presence.

Point Lookout Lighthouse still stands on the shore of Chesapeake Bay, but its duties were replaced by an automated light system after the Navy purchased the structure in 1965. The lighthouse remained occupied by residents up until 1981 but is now little more than a historical landmark and source of paranormal interest.

Tybee Lighthouse Station

Tybee Lighthouse Station, located in Georgia near the city of Savannah, is a popular tourist attraction and the home of some of the most famous ghosts in the area. The Lighthouse has been in operation since 1736, and its rich history has created a plethora of tales and legends about the hauntings that take place there.

The Tybee Island Light Station is said to be one of America's most intact light stations as the 5-acre site still has all the historic buildings still on the property. The lighthouse however has had an interesting history getting to its now resting place. The first one was 90 feet tall and is thought to be the tallest building of its day. Unfortunately, it was also built too close to the shore and in 1741 was washed away by a big storm.

In March of 1742, the second lighthouse was completed and with an addition of a 30-foot pole on top of the 90-foot structure, it now stood 124 feet tall and led

Oglethorpe to say "was much the best building in America". Again, however, they did not move it back enough and the ocean looked to take it. In 1773 the third lighthouse was built that now stood 100 feet tall. In 1790 Georgia ratified the Constitution and the lighthouse and surrounding land were given to the US Government.

In 1857, an 8-foot-tall Fresnel Lens was installed removing the 16 lamps that were used for light before it. It was this light that doomed the third lighthouse as the Confederates in nearby Fort Pulaski thought the lens was too bright and would aid the Federal Forces so ordered the lighthouse burned to the ground in 1861

In 1866 the fourth and current lighthouse was built and the first 60 feet was constructed with the original 1773 foundation. The current lighthouse is 150 feet tall and is topped by a 9 ft. Fresnel Lens. It took three keepers to man the lighthouse until its conversion to electricity in 1933. George Jackson became the last light keeper until he died in 1948.

The first ghost of the Tybee Lighthouse Station is known as "The Gray Lady." She is said to be the spirit of a young woman who tragically died in a shipwreck near the lighthouse. Her ghost is said to haunt the lighthouse and nearby beach, where she can often be seen searching for her lost love.

The second ghost of the Tybee Lighthouse Station is the "Lightkeeper Ghost." This ghost is believed to be the spirit of a former lightkeeper who died in a fire at the station. He has been seen wandering the grounds late at night, still tending to the light.

The third ghost of the Tybee Lighthouse Station is the "Grey Ghost." This apparition is said to be the spirit of a Confederate soldier who died in the Civil War. He is said to haunt the grounds of the lighthouse, and can often be seen wearing a grey uniform.

The fourth ghost of the Tybee Lighthouse Station is the "Lady in White." This ghost is believed to be the spirit of a young woman who died in childbirth at the lighthouse. Her ghost is said to haunt the grounds of the lighthouse, and can often be seen wearing a white dress.

The fifth and final ghost of the Tybee Lighthouse Station is the "Lighthouse Ghost." This ghost is said to be the spirit of a former lighthouse keeper who died in an accident at the station. He is said to haunt the grounds of the lighthouse, and can often be seen tending to the light.

Tybee Lighthouse Station is one of the most haunted places in Georgia, and it continues to attract visitors from all over the world.

CHAPTER THREE
HAUNTED HOUSES

Mullins

Haunted America

Every neighborhood has one of those houses that gives you chills. They're rumored to be haunted, but no one knows for sure. The houses were once filled with life and energy. Now only the shell remains, with a brief remembrance of those who once fed life into it. They stand empty and alone, but are they what they seem? Or are the caretakers still there living in silence?

Haunted houses are a staple of horror stories and folklore around the world, but not all hauntings are created equal. A haunted house is a building that is said to be inhabited by ghosts, spirits, or other supernatural phenomena. These hauntings can be anything from minor disturbances to full-blown apparitions.

The most common type of haunted house is the traditional haunted house, where a ghost or spirit of a deceased person haunts the house and its inhabitants. Usually, this haunting is in the form of strange noises, apparitions, and other paranormal activity such as objects moving on their own. In some cases, the ghost or spirit may even manifest itself physically.

Some haunted houses may also be considered to be haunted by a more malicious entity, such as a poltergeist or demon. These entities will often cause havoc in the home, leaving objects moved, broken, or even destroyed.

Regardless of the origins, haunted houses fill us with fascination and curiosity.

McRaven House

The McRaven House is one of the most haunted places in Mississippi. It is said to be home to numerous ghosts and eerie phenomena. Located in Vicksburg, the house has seen its fair share of tragedy.

McRaven House was built in 1797 by Andrew Glass in a town called Walnut Hills, which is now Vicksburg, MS. During the Civil War era, it was known as the Bobb House, and it is listed on the National Register of Historic Places as such. McRaven got its current name from the street it is located on, which was formerly called McRaven Street, but is now Harrison Street. It is believed by many to be haunted, and has been called "the most haunted house in Mississippi."

The ghosts of McRaven House are said to be the spirits of those who died there during the Civil War. It is believed that many soldiers died in the house during the Battle of Vicksburg, and their ghosts remain in the house to this day. Witnesses have reported hearing loud noises, knocking sounds, and disembodied voices coming from the house.

Mullins

Reports of paranormal activity are spread throughout the house; the center of activity seems to be the middle bedroom upstairs. It is the room where Mary Elizabeth Howard died during childbirth. Her ghost has been seen in the corner of the room, and on the bed where she passed away. The bedside lamp in the room is reported to turn on and off, seemingly at will. Mary Elizabeth's ghostly apparition has appeared on the house's flying wing staircase, and in the dining room.

Not long after Leyland French had purchased the property, a tour guide was bringing a group through the house when one of the tourists asked if the piano in the parlor worked. The guide pressed a key to find that it did not work. When the group was exploring the bedrooms, the sound of a beautiful Waltz was heard from the piano in the parlor. The guide quickly made her way downstairs but found the room empty.

As time passed, the disturbances got worse the atmosphere became oppressive, as a new demonic presence seemed to roam the House. On one particular occasion, a door was slammed through its own volition on the hand of Mr. French, causing injury. On another occasion, the owner states that as he walked through the parlor, he was pushed to his knees from behind by an unseen entity. He then saw the ghost of former owner William Murray on the staircase. The atmosphere now is a benign one, although ghosts are still seen at the McRaven House.

The ghost of William Murray is still seen by visitors usually at the top of the flying wing staircase. Murray's wife and daughter's ghosts haunt the grounds of the house.

In addition to the ghosts of soldiers, there have been reports of a spectral woman in white who is seen wandering the grounds. Some say she is the ghost of a bride who died on her wedding day, while others believe she is the spirit of a woman who was killed in the house during the Civil War.

The McRaven House is also home to other paranormal phenomena. Reports of orbs, cold spots, and strange lights have been reported. There have also been reports of objects moving on their own, and doors and windows opening and closing without explanation.

A Haunting At Whaley House

Whaley House is one of the most haunted places in America. Located in Old Town San Diego, California, it has been the site of mysterious and unexplained occurrences for decades, earning it a reputation as one of the most haunted places in the United States.

Built in 1856, the Whaley House was originally constructed as a general store and granary. But tragedy struck in 1852 when the house burned down, killing the storekeeper and his daughter. After the fire, Thomas Whaley and his family moved into the house and it quickly became known as the Whaley House.

Thomas Whaley built the home itself; it was home to The Tanner Troupe who used it as a theater, and it was even the San Diego County Court House at one time.

During the 1960's many visitors claimed to see, feel, or hear different apparitions, the strange part is these are only seen during daylight hours, as the home is empty at twilight. The strange sightings are still around today and if you visit, you should watch for Yankee Jim. Yankee Jim was hung on the property before Mr. Whaley purchased the property and built his home. Yankee Jim still enjoys running all around the house with heavy footsteps.

Since then, the Whaley House has been the site of numerous paranormal activities, including the sightings of ghostly apparitions, strange noises, and even poltergeist activity. People have reported hearing disembodied voices, seeing apparitions, and feeling cold spots in the house. There have also been reports of items moving on their own, doors opening and closing by themselves, and even objects being thrown across the room.

The most famous spirit said to haunt the Whaley House is that of Thomas Whaley himself. People have reported seeing his apparition in the parlor and his ghostly laughter floating down the hallways. Mr. Whaley's ghostly appearance can be seen in the upstairs bedroom smoking a pipe, and walking around the house, and Mrs. Whaley has been seen rocking a baby, folding laundry, and tucking a child in bed. Therefore, the Whaleys are still at home keeping the house as they did in the 1800's.

In the garden, a little red-headed girl has been and she was even spotted playing with toys. This may be the ghost of the little girl who died after being strangled accidentally in the backyard with a clothesline.

Other eerie sounds such as children laughing and playing, a child crying, music and singing, and whistling have also been around since the 60's.

The Whaley House is also said to be home to a mischievous poltergeist known as "Yankee Jim" Robinson. It is said that he was a thief who was hanged on the property in 1852 and now haunts the house. Reports of his ghostly antics include doors opening and closing by themselves, objects moving around, and strange noises being heard.

For those brave enough to visit the Whaley House, it is said that they will experience something paranormal. Whether it's a ghostly apparition, a cold chill in the air, or objects moving on their own.

LeLaurie House

The LaLaurie House, in New Orleans, Louisiana is a historic building that is known for its haunted history and ghostly activity. The house was built in 1832 by Doctor Louis LaLaurie and his wife Delphine. The couple were known for their wealth and extravagance but were also known for their cruelty and mistreatment of their slaves.

It is said that the mistreatment was so severe that it resulted in several deaths. It is said the LaLauries conducted horrific medical experiments on their slaves, as well as torturing and killing them. These horrific acts were likely what led to the hauntings that have been experienced in the house.

Delphine was a known socialite in New Orleans and was very wealthy. Within the house, she kept many slaves and seemed incapable of doing anything for herself. It was a common joke that she had one slave for everything, including picking up her teacup.

It was in 1833 that the slaves of the woman began disappearing. One of them, Lia, was running away from LeLaurie as she screamed for help and looked for ways to escape. She found her way to the rooftop and when

LeLaurie caught up with her, she beat the slave. Still trying to escape, Lia continued to fight her and fell over the rooftop, plunging to her death. Although there were witnesses, LeLaurie hid Lia's body in a well on her property. The authorities found it however and forced her to sell her remaining slaves at auction. Even though she did this, LeLaurie's friends bought her slaves and gave them back to her.

On April 10, 1834, the fire department responded to a call from the LeLaurie house. When they arrived, they found a cook who had been tied up in the kitchen. She admitted that she started the fire on purpose, but only to call attention to what was going on in the house. She told them to go to the attic where there was more help needed. When the police joined the fire department and they went up to the attic, it was a gruesome sight. There were all of LeLaurie's victims. Some were brought there after they had been killed by her and others had the room as the last place they'd seen. One thing was true, they had all been tortured and died terrible deaths.

This time, her friends would not help her. It's believed that she ran to Paris and was killed by a wild bull. Others believe that she ran to Paris only to return to the States a short time later to live under her new name,

"Widow Blanque." Although it has never been known how many people she murdered in total, it's known that there were many. As the home was renovated, skeletons of some of her victims were found.

The house has served many purposes since that time. It was a girl's boarding school, a tenement, an antique shop, a bar, and more. Many who have lived there over the years reported seeing apparitions and hearing noises as well as screams.

Visitors to the LaLaurie House have reported seeing strange lights, hearing strange noises, and feeling the presence of spirits that are believed to be the ghosts of the slaves who were mistreated by the LaLauries. These ghosts are said to be seeking justice for the wrongs that were done to them.

LeLaurie herself has been the most reported ghost, one man even woke up one night to her choking him. One man who was one of LeLaurie's slaves, likes to meet people on the stairs before disappearing. Many of the other servants have also been encountered in the home, and there are photographs near the spot of Lia's death, showing orbs of light.

One of the most common experiences reported at the LaLaurie House is the feeling of being watched. People have reported feeling as though they are being followed by an invisible force, and some have even experienced being touched by something unseen.

Lemp Mansion

Lemp Mansion in St. Louis, Missouri is purported to be one of the most haunted places in the United States. The story of the Lemp Mansion ghost is a tragic one, involving the suicides of several members of the Lemp family.

The Lemp family owned and operated the Lemp Brewery, which was as large as ten city blocks and was of course the largest in St. Louis until the time of prohibition. No one knows exactly what caused the demise of the Lemp Brewery it is one of those unknown mysteries.

The first strange occurrence in the Lemp family was the death of Frederick Lemp, the favorite son and heir of William. He died mysteriously in 1901. William grieved for three years before he committed suicide in the bedroom with a gun to his head. Over time, there have been four suicides in the Lemp Mansion.

Strange happenings have plagued visitors, guests, and staff members throughout history. One such event is that of a painter who began to feel someone was watching him while he was working on restoring the ceilings alone in the mansion. Out of nowhere, someone called his name, and he left without giving himself time to clean his equipment.

Another is one of a waitress, who arrived early and noticed a customer sitting alone at one of the tables. She began to walk up to him, to see if she could help but when she got within a few feet, he disappeared.

Many people have reported strange paranormal activity in the mansion. Visitors to the mansion have reported hearing strange noises, seeing ghostly figures, and feeling an unexplainable presence.

One of the most famous stories of the Lemp Mansion ghost is that of the 'Blue Lady'. The Blue Lady is believed to be the ghost of a woman named Julia, who was the daughter of William J. Lemp. She died of an illness at the young age of 18. It is said that her ghost haunts the mansion and that her presence is felt by those who enter.

Other strange reports of the Lemp Mansion ghost include the sounds of a baby crying, doors opening and closing by themselves, and furniture moving on its own.

There have also been reports of ghostly figures standing in the windows of the mansion.

Today, the Lemp Mansion is open for tours and visitors can experience the spooky atmosphere for themselves. Whether or not the ghosts of the Lemp family are still lingering in the mansion, the story of the Lemp Mansion ghost will continue to fascinate people for years to come.

McPike Mansion

Perched over the town of Alton atop its highest point, Mount Lookout Park, historic McPike Mansion is a hotspot for paranormal investigators who claim to feel the presence of its original owners, Eleanor and Henry McPike, as well as other residents.

This once-beautiful mansion was home to Henry Guest McPike and his family. The mansion was their home for many years and is now said to be inhabited by many ghosts.

There are several legends and ghost stories about this home. It stood abandoned for several years and was left to be vandalized, until during an auction, it was purchased by Sharyn and George Luedke, in 1994.

Some believe the haunting of this house, dates back to before the house was built, with detections of Native American ghosts and a residue from a possible Underground Railroad stop.

Overall, more than 11 spirits have been experienced throughout the home. There have been reports of strange noises, doors opening and closing on their own, and the sound of a baby crying. Many visitors have seen apparitions of a woman in white and a man in a top hat.

The most famous ghost is that of Mary, the daughter of Henry and his wife Jennie. According to legend, Mary was born with a physical deformity and her parents kept her hidden away in the mansion. When she died at the age of 12, her spirit is said to still haunt the mansion.

Other ghosts said to haunt the mansion include a former servant of the McPike family and a Civil War soldier. Some visitors have also reported seeing a ghostly figure of a woman floating in the air.

Alton is considered one of the most haunted small towns in America, and other eerie spots include a Confederate prison, a school, and a church.

Myrtles Plantation

It is said that the Myrtles Plantation is haunted, with things going on such as footsteps on the stairs, hand prints in mirrors, odd smells, objects disappearing, and even death by poison, hangings, and gunfire.

Myrtles Plantation, located in St. Francisville, Louisiana, and said to be one of the most haunted places in America. The plantation was built in 1796 and has been home to many tragedies throughout its long history.

The house has been the spot of at least 10 murders. One such murder and ghost that appears more often, is the ghost of Chloe. Chloe was hung for murdering two girls with a poised birthday cake. Chloe was seeking revenge on her master's son-in-law, Clarke Woodruff. Her master was General Bradford.

Clarke Woodruff cut off Chloe's ear for the sin of eavesdropping. She got her revenge, by poisoning his children at their birthday party. It is said Chloe only intended to make the girls sick. She put the wrong amount of poison in the cake, resulting in their deaths.

In this house, there is still a mirror, which is said that you can see the murder victims in it, and if you look closely at the right side, you can see spots believed to be messages from the dead. When people take pictures of the mirror, there are hand prints on the inside, as if someone is trying to communicate from the inside of the mirror. When these prints first appeared, the owners tried to clean them off, but they could not be removed. They then tried replacing the glass but the little handprints returned.

Myrtles Plantation is a popular tourist destination, and many people come to investigate the paranormal activity said to occur there. The owners of the plantation offer ghost tours, and visitors can stay in the rooms that are believed to be haunted.

The Haunted Stranahan House

After the owner of Stranahan House, Frank Stranahan drowned himself in the river outside his home during the Great Depression. People claimed to have seen his ghost wandering around the property ever since. Years later, the sister of Frank's widow also passed away in the house due to bleeding from prematurely giving birth to a stillborn baby. Six entities are said to haunt the house, including a man named Albert, who passed away in the Stranahan House six months after he caught TB from a prostitute.

Now open for public tours, this home gives a unique insight into the history and culture of the early 1900s, as well as the chance to spot one of the ghosts, which are often seen moving about, randomly changing temperatures of the rooms, and rearranging objects and furniture.

Oak Alley Plantation

Oak Alley Plantation, located in Vacherie, Louisiana, has a long and storied history, with many visitors claiming to have experienced paranormal activity on the grounds. Reports of apparitions, strange noises, and other strange phenomena have long been associated with this iconic plantation. If you love old plantation homes along with spooky occurrences then you must visit Vacherie, Louisiana.

This old 1800s plantation was the home of Jacques and Josephine Pile Roman. Jacques loved his home; however, Josephine missed the thrill of high society in New Orleans. She often went back to New Orleans with her children, leaving her husband alone. He became ill and died of tuberculosis in 1848, alone on the plantation.

Their daughter, Louise was raised alongside the high society in New Orleans. One evening, a suitor who was a bit drunk tried to approach her. She was so disgusted that she ran and tripped over the iron frame of her hoop skirt. Her leg was cut severely and she developed gangrene. Her leg was removed. After, she did not feel worthy of marriage, so joined a convent in St. Louis, Missouri. She did return home later.

After several owners, Andrew and Josephine Stewart purchased the plantation and restored it to its original state in 1925. This restoration may have been the catalyst to anger the spirits of the former owners and those who died there.

These plantation ghosts do not seem happy and have shown their ideas through the events over the years. Among the incidents are a candlestick being thrown across the room by unseen hands, and crying can be heard throughout the home. Spirits that have been seen, felt, or heard including the ghost of a thin, young woman with long dark hair has been seen on the walkway, in many different rooms, and riding a horse across the estate grounds. This spirit is believed to be that of either Josephine or her daughter Louise.

Jacques Telesphore Roman III's ghost is also believed to have been seen as well. He was said to be wearing gray clothing and riding boots, appearing outside, close by the old kitchen. His face has also been seen in a mirror that sits in the attic.

Visitors have reported hearing voices and strange noises coming from the plantation's many outbuildings. There have been reports of furniture moving by itself, and of doors opening and closing on their own. Some visitors have even reported the sounds of children playing in the distance.

The most commonly reported paranormal activity at Oak Alley Plantation is the presence of a ghostly figure near the entrance. This figure is believed to be the spirit of a former slave, believed to have been murdered on the property many years ago. It is said that the figure will appear near the entrance and then quickly disappear.

Phillips Mansion

The Phillips Mansion is an iconic structure located in the heart of downtown Spokane, Washington. Built in 1890 by local businessman William Phillips, the mansion has been the site of paranormal activity for decades. Witnesses have reported a variety of supernatural occurrences, ranging from odd noises to full-fledged apparitions.

This mansion is a two-story building in the Georgian Revival style, which is complete with gaslight fixtures and furnishings from the period including 19th-century sculptures and paintings.

The home was originally built in 1864 with eight rooms while the kitchen was placed in a shed nearby. As the years went by, new owners added more rooms.

In 1880, the home was purchased by James T. Phillips. His family lived in the mansion for 32 years. Then, in 1912, Dr. John F. Burleson purchased the home for his family. They lived there until 1934 when a strange fire forced them to leave.

In the 1940's, the mansion was a home for elderly women. The first documented supernatural event at the

Phillips Mansion occurred in the 1950s. An employee of the mansion reported seeing the apparition of an elderly woman. She was wearing a long dress and appeared to be in distress. This woman is believed to be the spirit of Mary Phillips, the wife of William Phillips, who died in 1921.

In 1952, investors purchased the mansion and transformed it into apartments. In 1973, two women who were renting an apartment on the second floor had a terrifying experience with beings from beyond the grave. Once again, the mansion was sold, this time to private owners, Ward Paul and Chuck Schwander. These men restored the mansion to its beautiful grandeur.

The first recorded frightful experience was during the time the mansion was used as apartments. One of the young women awoke in the middle of the night in 1972, with a large head of a young blond-haired man floating above her near the ceiling. The head floated across the room smiling down at her as it disappeared. Another experience involved a blinding light that filled her room. Finally, in 1973, a terrifying evening happened, which had the two girls packing and leaving their apartment for good.

The same girl who had witnessed the above occurrence awoke feeling someone was lying beside her in her bed. When she turned toward the person, she saw a very old, thin, wrinkled lady lying beside her. She could hear the woman breathe, and could see by her face she was in terrible pain. The young girl screamed and ran from the room. When her roommate came to see, the only thing left was the impression of where the old lady had been on the bed.

The mansion was purchased by Ward and Chuck. It was shortly afterward, that Chuck heard footsteps on the staircase that came up the stairs, down the hall, and stopped just outside his bedroom room. When he opened the door, he saw nothing. Ward also had an experience when unseen hands pulled his big toe one evening, while he was lying in bed reading.

Throughout the years, numerous other paranormal events have been reported at the Phillips Mansion. People have heard unexplained footsteps, voices, and other unexplained noises. Objects have been known to move around on their own, and some have even reported seeing shadowy figures lurking in the shadows. One of the most well-known spirits believed to haunt the Phillips Mansion is that of a little girl, believed to be the daughter of Mary and William Phillips.

In addition to the spirits, many visitors to the Phillips Mansion have also reported feeling an overwhelming feeling of unease or dread while inside. This feeling is often attributed to a negative energy present in the house, which some believe may be the result of a past tragedy.

Edgar Allen Poe's House

Edgar Allen Poe, the master of the macabre, was known for his horror and mystery stories. But did you know he may have had some real-life experience with the supernatural? Rumor has it, that his old house is haunted by a few of his ghostly companions.

Poe's home in Baltimore, Maryland, is said to be haunted by the author's ghost, as well as the ghosts of his beloved cat, Catterina, and his wife, Virginia. Reports of these spectral visitors have been circulating for years, and people who have visited the house have claimed to have seen strange lights and heard strange noises.

The small house is two and a half stories and is a brick-row house. During his stay there, Poe lived in a small attic room that the average adult could not stand up in. Poe's aunt, Marie Clemm rented the house in 1832, two years after it was built. When she moved in, she took Poe with her, along with Poe's grandmother and two of his cousins. One of these cousins was Virginia Clemm, whom he married later in life. Poe lived there until 1835.

The Edgar Allen Poe Society of Baltimore took over the house in 1941 after it was nearly torn down. It became open to the public and is run by Jeff Jerome, who was been the curator since 1977. One of the many points of interest in the house is a painting of Poe's wife taken from her corpse.

Many different sightings of hauntings and strange happenings have been talked about over the years. It's common for doors and windows to open and close by themselves. In 1968 a neighbor of the house called the police after seeing a light move throughout the darkened house late at night. The police arrived and noticed the light move from the first floor, up to the second, and then into the attic but when they entered the house, they didn't find anyone there.

The ghost of Edgar Allen Poe is said to be seen wandering the halls of the house, as if in search of something. Some have claimed to have seen him in the library, while others have seen him in the study. He is said to have a sad and melancholy look about him as if he is searching for something he can never find.

The ghost of Poe's cat, Catterina, is said to haunt the kitchen. She is said to be seen perched on the counter or wandering around the room. Some believe she is searching for her master as if she is trying to find a way to be reunited with him.

The ghost of Virginia, Poe's wife, is said to haunt the bedroom. It is said that she appears in the doorway of the bedroom, looking sad and lonely. It is said that she appears in the same spot each night; as if she is waiting for someone to come and take her away.

These are just a few of the ghosts that are said to haunt the house of Edgar Allen Poe. Whether they are real or just stories, the fact remains that the house of Edgar Allen Poe is said to be haunted. Whether you believe it or not, the stories of the ghosts remain and will continue to fascinate people for years to come.

Today, the house stands as not only a museum but also as a frightening landmark. Some have also said that Poe's ghost haunts the entire town.

Shirley Plantation

Shirley Plantation, Virginia, is the oldest family-owned business in the United States, having been in operation since 1613. But it's not just the rich history that makes Shirley Plantation unique—it's the ghosts. The plantation is reportedly haunted by the spirits of several of its former inhabitants, including a former slave, a Revolutionary War soldier, and a young girl.

The home was originally built by Edward Hill III, for his daughter Elizabeth, although his sister Martha, also stayed there for some time. Martha later traveled to England and while there, met an Englishman whom she married and lived with in England. However, she left behind a few things, including the portrait of a woman was very striking. Although no one quite knows why, the woman in the portrait over time became known as 'Aunt Pratt.'

Martha eventually passed away, but the portrait remained in the house. It was hung in the third-floor bedroom in 1858, when the family members in the house, heard a very loud rocking noise from that room. Going into the bedroom they saw the portrait rocking very hard against the wall where it hung. Not knowing what would cause it to do so, the family moved it into the attic. Again, there in the attic, the rocking became much, much worse. Word soon got out about the possessed portrait that resided in the Shirley Plantation. Not long afterward the Civil War broke out.

During the war, the plantation was turned into a hospital for wounded soldiers. During this time, Aunt Pratt's activity went unnoticed. When the war ended, Aunt Pratt was brought down to the first floor, where the portrait was still for a time. Eventually, she grew restless and the rocking returned. This time, the painting was moved to Martha's second-floor bedroom, where the painting seemed content and did not move for some time.

That portrait was part of an exhibit at Rockefeller Plaza in New York. However, Aunt Pratt was so discontent there that she began shaking so much, that she was immediately taken out of the exhibit and placed in a crate to be shipped back to the family. Workers claimed to have heard crying and rocking coming from inside the crate that the portrait was placed in. The next morning, the portrait was found lying outside of its crate, in the storage room.

The most famous of Shirley Plantation's ghosts is the Lady in Blue, who is believed to be the spirit of a former slave. According to legend, she was a housekeeper for the Hill family, who owned the plantation in the 19th century. She was a well-liked and respected member of the family, and after her death, her spirit was said to linger in the house. Visitors and staff have reported seeing the Lady in Blue in the dining room, hallways, and even outside in the gardens.

Another of Shirley Plantation's ghosts is the Revolutionary War soldier. According to legend, this soldier was a member of the Hill family who died while fighting in the war. He has been seen near the cemetery, and some visitors have reported hearing his voice in the darkness.

The final ghost of Shirley Plantation is a young girl, who is believed to be the daughter of a former owner. She is said to have died suddenly at a young age, and her spirit has been seen wandering the grounds of the plantation.

Shirley Plantation is a place full of history and mystery, and the stories of these ghosts only add to the intrigue.

The Ghosts Of Peyton Randolph House

Built in 1715 and restored in the 1900s, the Peyton Randolph House is one of the oldest homes in Virginia and one of the most haunted.

The Peyton Randolph House, located in Williamsburg, is an 18th-century Georgian mansion with a long and storied history. This iconic property has seen its share of battles, fires, and even ghosts. It is believed that the house is haunted by the ghost of its original owner, Peyton Randolph, a prominent political leader in colonial Virginia.

Peyton Randolph was born in 1721 in Williamsburg, Virginia. He was a lawyer, congressman, and later the first president of the Continental Congress. It was in 1770 that he purchased the house, which he used as a summer residence. Unfortunately, he died in 1775, and his wife moved back to their home in England.

The house has been the site of several battles during the Revolutionary War, including a battle in 1781 that saw the house set on fire. The original house was destroyed and rebuilt in the 19th century. It has since been restored to its original grandeur and is now a museum.

It's said that a slave named Eve cursed the house in retribution for cruel treatment; from then on, many people died on the property, including a Civil War soldier with a mysterious illness, a boy who fell from a tree, a girl who fell from a window, and two men who shot and killed each other during a heated argument.

These tragic incidents seem to have had a lasting effect on the house; over the years, visitors have reported hearing strange voices, seeing objects move on their own, and being touched or pushed.

The ghost of Peyton Randolph is said to haunt the mansion. Visitors have reported seeing the specter of a man in 18th-century clothing walking through the rooms of the house. Others have reported hearing the sound of a man's voice calling out from the upper floors.

In addition to the ghost of Peyton Randolph, there have been reports of other paranormal phenomena at the house. Visitors have reported hearing strange noises, seeing lights flickering, and even feeling a cold chill in the air.

The Peyton Randolph House is a unique piece of American history, and its ghosts are a reminder of the past.

Henniker House

New Hampshire is home to a number of haunted places, and one of the most famous is the Henniker House in Henniker. Built in 1776 by Colonel William Henniker, the house has a long and storied history, and many believe it is haunted by several entities.

Henniker House can be found on a hill overlooking the town of Henniker in the southwest part of New Hampshire on Highway 114. This home is now privately owned however, if you just mention Ocean Born Mary, the locals will tell you the story about this infamous ghost resident.

Mary Wallace at one time owned the home on the hill. Some locals say that Mary never leaves her home and is still living there even after her death.

Mary received her nickname "Ocean Born" Mary as her mother gave birth to her on an Irish immigrant ship. Pirates attacked the ship shortly after her birth. The pirate Don Pedro asked her mother to name her in honor of his mother Mary. The mother did as he asked; therefore, the pirate spared the ship, its belongings, and all the passengers.

The ship sailed into Boston and Mary's parents decided to call Londonberry, New Hampshire their home. This is where Mary grew up, married a man by the name of Wallace, and gave birth to four sons. After the birth of their fourth son, Wallace passed away.

The pirate Don Pedro retired from piracy and built a mansion on 6,000 acres in Henniker, New Hampshire. When he heard the news that Mary was a widow, he invited her to live with him. Mary agreed to his offer and married Don Pedro. She and her sons lived very happily with the ex-pirate.

However, life was not to end happily for Mary. She found her husband dying in the garden from a knife wound. He requested to be buried under the hearthstone in the kitchen, and Mary agreed to his wish. Mary lived in the home until she died in 1814 at the age of 94.

Several visitors to the home state they have seen a red-haired woman about six feet tall with beautiful green eyes standing by the upstairs bay windows and on the central staircase. Others have seen the same ghost throwing something down the well. Others still claim to see Mary riding throughout the countryside in a ghostly coach with ghostly horses.

Many more stories float around about Mary and when she has been seen in the town of Henniker.

Haunted America

CHAPTER FOUR
HAUNTED HOTELS

Throughout America, there are various haunted hotels. In days past, people would travel from place to place without any fear of encountering a ghost. However, as time has passed, more and more reports of occurrences have been reported in an ever-increasing number of hotels across the world.

These haunted hotels have become something of a fascination for those looking for a scary experience. The most common type of haunting reported in hotels is that of guests reporting the feeling of a presence, or hearing strange noises. Others have reported objects moving by themselves, doors opening and closing on their own, and objects disappearing and reappearing.

In some cases, it is more sinister, with reports of feeling a sense of dread, being watched, and being touched by an unseen entity. The hauntings are attributed to a restless spirit who is stuck in the hotel and unable to move on.

Whatever the cause of the hauntings, it is clear that these hotels are not for the faint of heart.

The Strange Case of Kate Morgan

The strange case of Kate Morgan has been a source of mystery for over a century. In 1892, Kate Morgan was found dead on the beach of the Hotel del Coronado in San Diego, California. She had checked in under the name of Lottie A. Bernard.

The police investigation determined that she had died of a self-inflicted gunshot wound to the head and that she had been dead for four days before her body was found. However, there were many strange details surrounding her death that made the case difficult to solve.

The Hotel del Coronado opened in 1888 in the city of Coronado, California, just across the bay from San Diego. It was the largest resort hotel in the world upon first opening, and the first resort to use electrical lighting.

On November 24, 1892, Kate Morgan checked in to the hotel, in room 304. She claimed she was there to meet with her brother, a doctor, who was treating her for stomach cancer. Five days after checking in, Morgan was found dead on the steps of the hotel leading down to the beach, of a self-inflicted gunshot wound.

However, there are some inconsistencies in the official account of Kate Morgan's death. For example, the bullet found in her head did not match the gun that was found in her room. Additionally, some witnesses claim to have seen a man running away from the hotel on the night of Kate's death.

As a result of these inconsistencies, some people believe that Kate Morgan's death was not a suicide, but rather a murder. However, there is no evidence to support this theory, and Kate Morgan's death remains a mystery to this day.

Morgan's ghost is thought to continue to haunt the Del Coronado to this very day. She has been seen wandering the hotel's halls, sitting in the hotel's lobby, and even appearing in the hotel's rooms. Some guests have reported hearing her footsteps or feeling her presence in their rooms.

In 2010, the Hotel del Coronado conducted a paranormal investigation with the help of a team of experts. The team found evidence of paranormal activity in several areas of the hotel, including the room where Kate Morgan died. The team also captured footage of a mysterious figure that they believe could be the ghost of Kate Morgan.

Bullock Hotel

Bullock Hotel, located in Deadwood South Dakota, has a reputation of being one of the most haunted hotels in the United States. Built in 1894, the Bullock Hotel was once the most luxurious in town and served as the headquarters of Sheriff Seth Bullock. Today, the hotel is said to be haunted by the spirits of those who once frequented the hotel, including Sheriff Bullock himself.

Seth Bullock and a partner named Star built an upscale hotel in Deadwood, which of course, was still very wild at the time. When this hotel burned to the ground in 1876, Seth and his partner once again built another hotel. This time it was over a fireproof store and warehouse that had survived two burns. The Bullock Hotel was opened in 1895. Seth lived in this hotel until he died in 1919, in room 211. He was buried on the trail to White Rocks above Mount Moriah Cemetery.

Since the death of Seth Bullock, his hotel has seen many renovations, but the spirits never seem to leave. The recorded manifestations began around 1989. No one is for sure if they were there before this time, or if something during this time disturbed, the ghosts that call Bullock Hotel their resting place.

The main spirit to haunt the Bullock Hotel is believed to be that of the former owner, Sheriff Bullock. Witnesses have reported seeing the figure of a man in a top hat and long coat walking around the hotel late at night. Others have heard a mysterious voice calling out from the shadows.

The hotel also has a long history of paranormal activity. Witnesses have reported hearing strange noises, seeing shadows, feeling cold spots, and experiencing the sensation of being watched. Some people have even seen objects move on their own.

The Bullock Hotel is also said to be haunted by the ghosts of former visitors. Several guests have reported seeing the ghosts of people in the halls and rooms of the hotel. These apparitions are said to be that of former guests who stayed at the hotel, and some have even been seen in the restaurant and bar.

The Bullock Hotel is also known lights flickering, and even doors opening and closing by themselves. Many of these occurrences have been attributed to the hotel's paranormal activity.

Haunted Omni Mount Washington Resort

While the Mount Washington Hotel in Bretton Woods is a relaxing wooded getaway, it's also home to some seemingly benevolent spirits. Guests and staff have reported seeing an elegantly dressed woman wandering the hotel in the off-season and even captured her once in a summer staff photo.

The sightings and supernatural events are attributed to the ghosts of the original owners of the hotel, who seem to enjoy keeping watch over their beloved property.

Caroline Foster, whose husband, railroad tycoon Joseph Stickney, built the grand resort, was a long-time inhabitant. The property was built with special accommodations for her, including an indoor swimming pool and private dining room.

Ever since its opening, and long since she passed, many guests have continued to report sightings of the regal Caroline, an elegant woman in Victorian dress often spotted in the hallways. There are light taps on doors when no one is outside, items suddenly disappear and then reappear in the exact place they were lost.

Other famous spirits to haunt the resort include, the "ghost of the grand staircase." This ghost is said to be the spirit of a former bellboy who died on the stairs in the early 20th century. Guests have reported a ghostly figure ascending and descending the grand staircase, and some have reported hearing voices coming from the stairwell.

Other hauntings at the Omni Mount Washington Resort, include the ghost of a woman in a white dress, who is said to be the spirit of a guest, who died at the hotel in the early 1900s. Guests have reported seeing her in the hallway, walking down the stairs, and even standing in the corner of their rooms.

The Resort is also said to be haunted by the spirit of a former owner, Joseph Stickney. who died in the hotel in 1911. Guests have reported seeing his apparition in the lobby, in the dining room, and in the halls.

Guests of the resort have also reported seeing lights flickering in empty rooms, hearing disembodied voices in the hallways, and feeling a chill in certain areas of the hotel.

The Crescent Hotel

If you ever travel to Eureka Springs, Arkansas, you will notice a historic hotel and spa on the edge of the West Mountain. This hotel was built in 1886 and today is one of the most famous places to stay in all of Eureka Springs.

The hotel, when it was built, was a one-of-a-kind architectural style with 18-inch walls, overhanging balconies, and towers, and the most unique item in the hotel was the stone fireplace set in the lobby. When the hotel was finished it came in at a cost of $294,000. The grand opening was held on Mary 20, 1886.

The lavish rooms and beautiful landscape were not enough to keep visitors coming, and from 1908 to 1924, this unique and beautiful hotel became the Crescent College and Conservatory for Young Women. It was only during the summer months when it was used as a resort. It was not long before the college could not maintain the upkeep, and the expense became just too much. After 16 years, the college closed.

Through the years, Crescent Hotel has gone under many different names and identities, even a cancer hospital at one time, however, the ghosts that roam the halls never change.

In 2002, renovations were completed and the magnificent hotel was completely restored to its original state. It may be the most beautiful hotel in all of the Ozarks, but it is also claimed to be the most haunted.

Many ghostly appearances have been seen throughout the Crescent Hotel and Spa. While other hotels have one or two ghosts or spirits, this hotel has more than 40. The most famous of these is Dr. Norman Baker, a charlatan, who ran a fraudulent cancer-cure hospital in the hotel in the 1930s.

Dr. Baker was a conman who promised patients a cure for their cancer, but instead, he bilked them out of their money. He was eventually caught and sent to prison for his crimes. But his spirit still lingers in the hotel, and he is said to roam the halls late at night, opening and closing doors.

An Irish stonemason called "Michael" by the staff is seen more often than any other apparition. He is believed to be one of the original stonemasons who aided in the construction of the hotel in 1866. The legend states that while Michael was working on the roof, he fell when he lost his footing. He enjoys playing with the lights, the television, and the doors and when he is really mischievous, he loves to stick his hand out of the bathroom mirror in Room 218.

On the third floor of the hotel, you may just get a glimpse of a nurse dressed all in white pushing a gurney down the hall. She is only seen after 11 p.m., the time when cancer patients who had passed away were moved from their rooms.

Another spirit, Theodora is a cancer patient that lives in Room 419. She has only been seen by housekeepers. She is said to introduce herself and then vanish.

Other ghosts in the hotel include a little girl who is often seen in the lobby playing with her ball, a woman in white who is believed to be a former maid and a man in a top hat who is thought to be a former resident of the hotel.

There have been numerous reports of strange noises, lights flickering, and objects moving on their own. Guests have reported hearing footsteps coming from empty rooms, the sound of a baby crying, and the smell of cigar smoke in the air.

The owners of the hotel have embraced the ghost stories and even offer ghost tours for those brave enough to explore the haunted halls.

The Ghost Of Foley House Inn

Savannah, Georgia, is arguably the most haunted place in America. The Foley House Inn bed and breakfast stands on the very spot where a home was destroyed by the Great Savannah Fire of 1889 and a new one was built in 1896. According to local lore, the house is haunted by the ghost of a man who was killed there.

Legend has it that one night a suspicious boarder attempted to strangle Ms. Foley. Unable to scream, she beat the attacker over the head with a candlestick and inadvertently killed him. In exchange for free rent, a guest disposed of the body.

Years later, Foley confessed to the killing on her deathbed but never revealed the location of the body, and most people dismissed the claim. However, during a renovation in 1989, human skeletal remains were discovered in the walls and, ever since, guests have reported seeing a man wearing a top hat in the garden at night, hearing strange noises, and feeling sudden rushes of air. Locals refer to the entity as "Wally."

Gold Hill Hotel

Gold Hill Hotel can be found on Highway 342 close to the Gold Hill mines about one mile south of Virginia City, Nevada. It is steeped in history and legend, and it also comes with a few ghost stories. The hotel, built in 1862, is just a few miles from Virginia City. It has seen many different owners throughout its history and has also acquired some ghostly inhabitants that have been the source of many strange stories.

The original hotel and saloon was built in 1859 and is considered to be the oldest hotel in the state of Nevada. The two-story hotel at the time of its creation was known as the Riese House until the property was leased by Horace Vessy in 1862. At this time, Vessey added a 3-story building adjacent to the original hotel.

The hotel throughout the years has had many faces including a hotel, a boarding house, and a private residence. Today, the western hotel and saloon is still serving lunch and dinner. The hotel is popular with the living and the spirits of those who once passed through there.

Room 4 has the ghost of a young woman, known as Rosie. When you walk into the room, you will notice the smell of roses, such as perfume worn during the Western days. She also enjoys turning the lights on and off. She seems to take pleasure in moving things around including guest's personal belongings.

In room 5 you will find a ghost only known as William. He is believed to be one of the 47 miners who died in a fire in Yellowjacket Mine. Many people smell tobacco as they walk into the room. William is known as a prankster. He loves to lock the door to his room and keep guests out.

The upstairs hall has become the home to the sounds of ghost children running and giggling. Along with the playful antics, there is the smell of chocolate chip cookies.

Golden North Hotel

Legend has it that this former hotel is home to a few ghosts. Since the Alaskan gold rush years, the Golden North Hotel has been a popular destination for tourists and locals alike, but it is also said to be haunted by a few spirits from the past.

In 2002, The Golden North Hotel returned to its original use; as a commercial building, but its history lives on. The Golden North Hotel in Skagway, Alaska is known for its residence ghosts in rooms 14 and 23. Some guests staying in either room felt like they were ill with a faint feeling coming over them, while others felt like they were having a hard time breathing, as you would if you had pneumonia.

Room 23 is where a woman stayed waiting for her husband to return from mining for gold. She lived there pretty much in hiding from the scoundrels that lived in the area that would prey upon others and rob them of any gold they might have. She died of pneumonia before her husband ever returned.

The entity that is believed to haunt room 23. Was seen as a young pretty woman called Mary by all the staff.

Mary appeared not only as a glimpse but also fully to chambermaids and maintenance men. She was been seen staring out of the window of room 23 waiting for her husband to come back.

Mary was not afraid of the living, and enjoyed having her photo taken, as she was seen in a photo of a singer in the area. After the picture was developed, Mary could be seen standing right beside him.

Room 14 was another room that Mary seemed to like. She has visited this room quite frequently.

Goldfield Hotel

Goldfield, Nevada, is said by psychics, to be one of seven existing portals to the other side. It is there, at the Goldfield Hotel, where one terrible thing would happen that would forever change the corridors, and one room in particular, Room 109. The hotel was built in 1908 and was considered to be one of the most beautiful and luxurious hotels in Nevada at the time.

After the hotel was built, it was sold and purchased by George Winfield, who was a very prominent figure and considered to be a great businessman with many political, financial, and otherwise powerful connections. Shortly after he made his large purchase, Winfield started to have a romance with a prostitute. Due to his standing in the community and the career in which she made her living, Winfield wanted the affair to be kept secret. Shortly after, the prostitute became pregnant!

Whether or not George Winfield continued with the affair, is not known, but it can be told that the prostitute tried desperately to remain a part of her lover's life, as she ended up in Room 109, chained to the radiator. She was already very far along in her pregnancy, and it's thought that Winfield himself put her up there. She remained there until she had her baby, moments after its birth, was ripped from its mother's hands. It was then thrown down the chute, that was the way to the abandoned gold mine where the hotel had been built. It's also unknown whether the prostitute was murdered after having her baby taken away from her, or whether she was simply left to die in Room 109.

Many tourists have often said they have found that while taking pictures throughout the building, Room 109 was the only room in which their cameras would not work. Psychics have also investigated the room and found that there was paranormal activity there, and a woman with long, flowing hair could be seen floating near the ceiling. Perhaps the owner, George Winfield, has a guilty conscience, as his spirit can also often be felt around the building.

The Plains Hotel

The Plains Hotel in Cheyenne, Wyoming has been the site of many ghostly sightings and paranormal activity since it opened in 1911. The hotel was originally built as a luxury hotel to help accommodate the many travelers who were coming to Cheyenne from the East Coast and other parts of the country. Although the hotel has been renovated several times throughout the years, many of its original features remain intact, including the mysterious staircase and the attic, which are believed to be the sites of some of the most intense paranormal activity.

"The Magic City of the Plains," as Cheyenne, Wyoming was known in the late 1800s seemed like the perfect place to build a luxury hotel, according to the Industrial Club in 1909. The decision was made at a dinner party when Thomas Heaney, the club's President, announced that Cheyenne needed something elegant and modern to spruce up the town a bit.

An architect by the name of William Dubois designed the hotel quickly and construction began in June 1910. By March of the next year, the Plains Hotel was ready for its grand opening. The hotel soon became known as a place of extravagance. However, the hotel was soon to be the eternal resting place of a couple of its guests.

This story is about a young woman named Rosie, and her new groom. The couple had come to Cheyenne on their honeymoon and had chosen to stay in the Plains Hotel. The groom was nervous and grew restless one evening. He decided to go downstairs to the bar for a drink. It was there, that he struck up a conversation with a prostitute.

Rosie, being alone in her room, grew restless as time passed, and decided to go find him. Stopping in the bar's entrance, she her husband, and the prostitute sitting at the bar, being fun and flirty with each other. She watched both of them for several minutes until they left and went upstairs to the woman's room on the fourth floor.

Enraged, she followed them both and after they had been inside the room for another several minutes, she burst through the door, to find them in bed together. Engulfed with rage, she shot both of them with a gun that belonged to her new husband. Fleeing the scene, she returned to her room, where she killed herself.

Since that fatal night, guests and employees of the hotel have been witness to the three ghosts. Housekeeping staff have said that they can hear sounds coming from the room that Rosie stayed in. The sounds are of both laughing and crying. When the door is opened, no one is inside. Rosie is also said to be seen walking around the second floor in a long blue gown.

The groom doesn't stay too long in one place. Perhaps he is overcome with guilt, and that makes him restless. He is most often seen on the fourth floor, where he was shot. Other times, he is seen at times in the basement. He is seen wearing early 1900s formal clothing.

The prostitute still lingers as well. She is seen wearing a short red, lacy dress. One Halloween, the hotel was decorated for Halloween. Two mannequins were placed in the lobby. One was dressed as a bride and the other was a groom. One day when an employee was in the lobby, they saw the ghost of the prostitute. As soon as the employee noticed the ghost, the mannequin that was dressed like a bride fell to the ground. The employee had barely enough time to see the mannequin fall before the ghost was gone.

The Plains Hotel still hosts many visitors today. It retains its historic appeal but offers amenities to satisfy today's modern clients. Although these guests are temporary, three guests from the past will most likely stay at the hotel forever.

Ghosts Of The Bisbee Arizona Copper Queen Hotel

The Copper Queen Hotel in Bisbee, Arizona is one of the most haunted buildings in the state. Built in 1902, this historic hotel is said to be home to several restless spirits that have been roaming its halls for decades. The hotel has a long history of unexplained paranormal activity, from mysterious lights and sounds to full-fledged apparitions.

Arizona's oldest hotel still in operation today, was built to accommodate the traffic brought to town by mines rich with copper, lead, and silver. Every mining town has its ghost stories, but the Copper Queen Hotel has an unusually high number of tales and strange happenings.

One well-known story surrounding the old luxury hotel was that of the suicide of a woman, who died in her 30s named Julia Lowell. People said she was a prostitute and used the hotel for her sexual clients. Sadly, she fell in love with one of her clients, and when she told him how she felt, he no longer wanted to see her. Julia took her own life there at the hotel. Guests and staff, say that they feel her presence on the second and third floors of the west side of the building. Male staff and guests have reported hearing a female voice whispering in their ear. She has also been seen dancing provocatively at the foot of the stairs.

It is also said the ghosts of several children still roam the halls. The spirits of some of the ghosts who worked there, also haven't left the building, and still roam the grounds they experienced in life.

The Renaissance Mayflower Hotel

The Mayflower Hotel in Washington, D.C. is one of the oldest and most storied hotels in the United States. But it's not just the hotel's rich history that makes it unique–it's also home to some very special guests: ghosts.

The Mayflower has been in business since 1925 and has been the host of many important political and cultural figures, including presidents, diplomats, and celebrities. It's no surprise then that some of these famous visitors have left their mark in the form of ghostly sightings. The most famous of these is the "Crying Lady", a woman in a white dress who appears to be weeping and has been seen by many guests over the years.

This hotel was the location of an inaugural ball that would be missing the guest of honor, President Calvin Coolidge. That year the President's inaugural ball was held on March 4, 1925 however, the President's son had just died tragically from blood poisoning and so, the President did not attend.

These days, the hotel sees some very strange things on Inauguration Day, like the lights have been known to flicker and dim at around 10:00 p.m. Some years, a plate of appetizers along with a glass of wine have also been left on the Grand Ballroom's balcony, although current staff did not place them there and those items weren't even served at the inauguration ball. Also, every January 20th, the elevator sits on the 8th floor and will not move to the lobby until 10:15 p.m.

President Coolidge is thought to be behind all of the strange occurrences that happen around the Renaissance Mayflower Hotel on Inauguration Day. Some like to say that the former President is still trying to make up for his absence at the party thrown in his honor.

The most active ghost in the Mayflower is believed to be a former employee by the name of Claude, who worked in the hotel for more than 20 years. He is said to be a friendly spirit, often seen in the lobby or the hallways, and sometimes even stopping to chat with guests.

Other spirits are said to haunt the Mayflower as well. A man in a tuxedo is often seen in the grand ballroom, and a little girl in a white dress has been spotted in the elevator. People have also reported seeing the ghost of a former president walking the halls, and the ghost of an old manager on the fifth floor.

The Roosevelt Hotel

The Hollywood Roosevelt Hotel in Los Angeles, California is rumored to be one of the most haunted hotels in the United States. It was built in 1927, and it has hosted many famous guests over the years, including Marilyn Monroe, Montgomery Clift, and Errol Flynn.

The most popular ghost that has been seen by guests is Marilyn Monroe. On the lower level of the hotel beside the elevators in the infamous mirror, that at one time resided in the room in which Marilyn Monroe slept. Many guests have seen Monroe's reflection in the mirror. She has also been seen close by her tomb at Westwood Memorial Cemetery.

Room number 928 was the favorite room of Actor Montgomery Clift during the three months of filming "From Here to Eternity" and his spirit can still be seen there today. Several guests have reported cold spots in the room, and one guest felt him pat her on the shoulder.

Other ghosts have been encountered in the Blossom Room where the first Academy Awards banquet was held. Others have felt the eerie cold spots, and have noted a ghost dressed in a white suit on the balcony above the mezzanine. As soon as they approach the ghost in white, he vanishes very quickly.

The hotel is said to be haunted by the ghosts of several of its former guests, including:

Marilyn Monroe: Monroe is said to haunt her former suite, room 1200. She is often seen in the mirror in the suite, or walking the halls of the hotel.

Montgomery Clift: Clift is said to haunt his former room, 928. He is often heard playing the trumpet or seen walking the halls of the hotel.

Errol Flynn: Flynn is said to haunt the hotel's Blossom Ballroom. He is often seen dancing in the ballroom or drinking at the hotel bar.

In addition to these specific ghosts, there have also been numerous reports of strange activity at the hotel, including:

Footsteps and voices are being heard in empty rooms

Lights turning on and off by themselves

Doors opening and closing by themselves

Apparitions being seen

Cold spots being felt

Strange odors being smelled

Some people believe that the ghosts of the former guests still haunt the hotel, seeking justice or revenge. Others believe that the ghosts of the hotel staff members or other individuals who lived or worked at the hotel still remain.

The Hollywood Roosevelt Hotel is still in operation today, and it is a popular tourist destination.

Lady in Red Ghost Of The Mizpah Hotel

Mizpah Hotel opened in 1907 as one of Nevada's first luxury hotels, complete with solid granite walls and Victorian-era décor, and it was fully restored in 2011. But the swanky hotel has a history as blood-red as its scarlet furnishings.

The Lady in Red Ghost of the Mizpah Hotel is one of the most famous hauntings in the United States. This is due to the numerous reports of paranormal activity within the hotel, as well as the strong presence of the Lady in Red.

The Mizpah Hotel was built in 1907 and quickly gained a reputation for being haunted. The hotel was host to many famous people, including the likes of Clark Gable, Marilyn Monroe, and the infamous Al Capone. It has also been the site of several reported hauntings, including the Lady in Red.

The Lady in Red is said to be a spirit that has been seen by guests, staff, and even the hotel's owners. She is said to haunt the fifth floor of the hotel and is described as a woman in a red dress. She is believed to be the spirit of a woman who was murdered in the hotel in the early 1900s.

Legend has it that a woman died on the fifth floor, and her soul never left the building. The "Lady in Red" now reportedly makes her presence known by whispering in men's ears and leaving pearls from her broken necklace on guests' pillows. The Mizpah honors her reputation by letting visitors stay in the Lady in Red suite and serving the Red Lady Bloody Mary at the hotel restaurant.

The story of the Lady in Red has been featured in numerous books, television shows, and films, and is one of the most iconic hauntings in the United States. Her presence at the Mizpah Hotel has made it one of the most popular tourist attractions in Tonopah, Nevada.

The Haunted Queen Anne Hotel

The Queen Anne Hotel in San Francisco is one of the city's most iconic and historical landmarks. Built in 1890, the hotel has a long and storied history, and it is also rumored to be one of the most haunted places in the city.

The Queen Anne is located in the city's historic Pacific Heights neighborhood, and the building itself is an architectural marvel. The exterior features ornate Victorian-style architecture, with a large wrap-around porch and intricate detailing. Inside, the hotel is full of old-world charm, with vintage furniture, period antiques, and a grand staircase.

When it was built in 1890, this Victorian hotel in San Francisco served as an etiquette school for girls. It's since been reborn as a 48-room hotel, although remnants of the building's past life still linger.

The ghost of Miss Mary Lake, the school's late headmistress, is said to haunt the hotel, particularly room 410 (her former office). Guests who stay in that room might wake up to find their clothes have been unpacked, or the blankets closely tucked around them in bed.

Haunted America

CHAPTER FIVE
HAUNTED HOSPITALS AND
ASYLUMS

For many, abandoned asylums, and closed-down hospitals are some of the spookiest locations to visit. Empty hospitals are eerie on their own, but even more so when you consider that spirits of the departed could be lurking around any corner, and haunting the hallways of the hospital they once resided

Hospitals and Asylums are often considered hot spots for paranormal activity, since countless people pass on in those facilities, often unexpectedly, which is one explanation for why many spirits still linger there, rather than crossing over.

Essex County Hospital

Ghost stories have been around for centuries, and they bring a sense of mystery and intrigue to the places they inhabit. There's something special about a place that's haunted by spirits that refuse to rest in peace. One such place is Essex County Hospital in New Jersey, which is reportedly haunted by the ghosts of former patients and staff.

In 1896, the city of Newark New Jersey purchased a large landmass in Cedar Grove, choosing this location to house the new Overbrook mental institution (later termed Essex County Hospital). Over the next several years, foundation after foundation was erected to house the mentally ill and criminally insane.

Over time, the facility declined and so did its practices. Patients were subject to torrential conditions and often violent treatment by the staff. Electro-shock therapy, pre-frontal lobotomies, diathermy, and hydrotherapy were extremely common. By the 1960s and 70s, anti-psychotic drugs became popularized, and the Essex County Hospital's patient population began dropping significantly. In 1990, the building was nearly empty of patients.

Finally, in 2007, the Essex County Hospital was closed and the grounds were converted into a county park spanning 90 acres. A number of the buildings were demolished but the main structures stand to this day. The level of paranormal activity at the Essex County Hospital is incredible, though it is little surprise when historians have reported more than 10,000 human deaths having taken place in the mental institution since its establishment over a century ago.

The most common reports of spiritual activity include the sound of a squeaky-wheeled gurney being rolled about the halls, ghostly apparitions appearing in various locations, audible if not loud footsteps coming from locations where no living being could be found, and voices ranging from faint whispers to spine-tingling screams.

Bartonville State Hospital

Bartonville State Hospital is known for its mysterious and haunted past. Located in Bartonville, Illinois, the hospital was built in the late 19th century as a mental health facility. It was in use until 1973 when it was shut down. Since then, it has become a popular spot for ghost hunters and paranormal investigators.

The hospital is believed to be haunted by the spirits of former patients and staff. Visitors to the hospital often report hearing strange noises, seeing shadows, and feeling a sense of dread in the air. People have also reported seeing apparitions of people in white gowns, as well as the ghostly figure of a nurse.

There are several theories as to why the hospital is haunted. One popular theory is that the ghosts are former patients who never made it out alive. Another popular theory is that the spirits of former staff members still linger in the hospital.

In recent years, the hospital has been featured in several documentaries and paranormal TV shows. It has also become a popular destination for ghost hunters and paranormal enthusiasts. The hospital is now open to the public for tours, giving visitors the chance to experience the history and mystery of the hospital for themselves.

Restless Spirits Of Kennebec Arsenal

Located in Augusta, Maine, the historic Kennebec Arsenal was built following the War of 1812. But for nearly 100 years of its history, the building served as the Maine State Hospital, later renamed the Augusta Mental Health Institute, remaining operational until 2004.

During its time as a hospital, more than 11,600 people died there, though there are no detailed reports of where their bodies were buried.

While the hospital has since closed, the former Arsenal has become a popular site for ghost hunters, and it has been said to be haunted by the restless spirits of its former occupants. There have been numerous reports of strange noises, unexplainable phenomena, and sightings of mysterious figures throughout the Arsenal. One of the most common ghost stories is that of a soldier who was killed during the Civil War and who is said to still haunt the Arsenal.

Other reports include the sounds of drums and marching feet, the appearance of lights in the windows, and the feeling of being watched by unseen eyes. Many believe that these spirits are those of the men and women who served at the Arsenal in its heyday.

Ghosts Of The Trans-Allegheny Lunatic Asylum

The Trans-Allegheny Lunatic Asylum was originally called the West Virginia Hospital for the Insane and is known for its dark history. It was built in 1864, but in the 1950s, the facility reached its peak, housing more than 2,400 patients—even though it was designed to hold only 250.

The severe overcrowding led to inhumane conditions, and patients started acting increasingly violent, from starting fires to attacking staff members. The site of hundreds of deaths, including suicides and murders.

The asylum finally closed in 1994, but the souls of some patients are said to linger. Some of the paranormal events reported by employees were the sounds of gurneys being pushed up and down the hallways. The electro-shock area has had reports of screams coming from it. Full body apparitions of patients as well as doctors have been claimed to be seen roaming the halls and rooms. Voices that have ranged from giggling and laughing to ominous warnings to leave the building have also been reported to be heard all around the facility.

Pennhurst State Hospital

Pennhurst State Hospital, located in Spring City, Pennsylvania, has a long and storied past. Originally opened in 1908 as the first state-run mental institution in Pennsylvania, the hospital gained notoriety for its dark and inhumane conditions. The hospital was eventually shut down in 1987 after a series of court battles.

It was originally known as the Eastern Pennsylvania Institution for the Feeble-Minded. It was a facility for people with mental and physical disabilities and almost since day one, was overfilled and facing problems of abuse. Today we know it as Pennhurst State School and long after it closed its doors for the last time in 1986, the people who died here still call this school home making it one of the most haunted places in America.

Pennhurst State School is said to be extremely active with paranormal activity. There have been reports of full-bodied apparitions, voices of people talking, screams of patients, doors slamming, and the uneasy feeling of constantly being watched.

The Pennhurst State School is currently closed to the public.

Elgin State Mental Hospital

The Elgin State Mental Hospital is a dark, malevolent institution that has housed and "treated" the criminally insane for over 150 years. For most of that time, the treatment for insanity was of a brutal, if not inhumane, nature. Under such circumstances, it's not hard to believe that the Elgin State Mental Hospital is one of Illinois' most haunted locations.

The hospital opened in 1872 and was originally known as the Northern Illinois Hospital and Asylum for the Insane. It was later renamed the Elgin Mental Health Center and has since been demolished. Throughout its history, the hospital has been the site of numerous tragic events, including patient abuse, deaths, and suicides.

It is widely believed that the Elgin State Mental Hospital Cemetery, located back behind the modern-day sports complex, was overused. The death rate was so high that up to 5 bodies were buried in each grave, with only the upper-most body's name being carved into the tombstone.

It's believed the spirits of the patients still haunt the grounds of the former hospital, and many visitors have reported strange phenomena. The claims include whispers, voices, and screams that could be heard in the night. Lights controlled themselves. Banging on the doors when no one was there. One past patient who spent 9 months of his teenage life within its walls, claims to have awoken in the night, being attacked in his bed by an unseen phantom slashing at his face. His door was locked and no one was in the room all night.

Puget Sound Mental Hospital

Puget Sound Mental Hospital is an abandoned psychiatric hospital in Washington State, that has become the focus of many ghost stories and paranormal activity. The hospital was built in the late 19th century and was used until its closure in 1973. Since then, it has become a popular destination for ghost hunters and paranormal enthusiasts.

Originally built in 1926, the mental hospital has quite a history. Some say the very first experimental lobotomies were performed there, which would have undoubtedly had irrevocable adverse effects on the unfortunate patients who underwent such trials.

Like most mental institutions operating in these times, Puget Sound Mental Hospital is said to be haunted by the maltreated, neglected, and overcrowded detainees who suffered, and many who died, within its walls. The fact that at least some of them were truly deranged to begin with doesn't help matters, as they return from the afterlife to walk the halls of the asylum.

Stories of strange and creepy occurrences at the hospital abound. Reports of ghostly figures, mysterious lights, and disembodied voices have been reported for over a century. Many believe that these occurrences are the result of the tragic and often violent events that occurred at the hospital.

Some of the more chilling stories include reports of a nurse being pinned to the wall by an unseen force, and of a ghostly figure that would walk the corridors of the hospital at night. Other reports include disembodied laughter, strange shadows, and the presence of an unknown entity.

The most famous ghost of Puget Sound Mental Hospital is that of an elderly lady who haunts the 4th floor, now closed off from the operational section of the institution. She manifests traversing the hall with her walker, and sometimes when she is not spectrally visible, her walker can still be heard scraping across the floor.

It's not hard to believe that the mental institution is haunted, considering its long and shady past.

.

Holy Cross Sanatorium

The Holy Cross Sanatorium in Ypsilanti, Michigan, is said to be haunted by many ghosts. The sanatorium, which was built in the late 1800s, has a long and storied history of treating the ill and injured. It was closed in the early 2000s, and since then, visitors to the abandoned building have reported seeing strange phenomena. Those who have ventured into the old sanatorium have reported seeing the apparitions of nurses and doctors who used to work there, as well as the ghosts of patients who once sought treatment there.

Originally established as a military base by the name of Camp Cody, the remains of the Holy Cross Sanatorium have quite a history of death, suffering, and ongoing mischief. They say the underground tunnels and last standing building of Holy Cross Sanatorium are haunted by the disgruntled ghosts of a century gone by.

Many of the visitors to the sanatorium claim to have experienced a feeling of uneasiness, and some have even reported feeling a sense of dread as they explore the abandoned building. Those who have encountered the strange phenomena often describe a feeling of being watched, as if something was lurking in the shadows.

CHAPTER SIX
HAUNTED PLACES AND
BATTLEFIELD GHOSTS

Haunted battlefields and places where traumatic events have happened are some of the most haunted locations in the world. Many people believe that the spirits of those who died in war linger in these places, creating a feeling of unease and fear.

Do places where violent deaths occur somehow absorb the events that have happened? Many people believe that this can happen. Haunted battlefields and places are some of the most haunted places in the world. Many people believe that the spirits of those who died in war linger in these places, creating a feeling of unease and fear.

In addition to battlefields, there are also haunted locations associated with conflict. Abandoned prisons, fortresses, and bunkers often have stories of spirits haunting the area. These places often have a dark history and many believe that the spirits of those who died in the conflict are still there, unable to move on to the afterlife.

It is difficult to explain why some locations are so haunted, but many believe that it is because of the strong emotions felt during the final moments of life. It is possible, that the energy of those emotions lingers in the area.

The Ghosts of Cheesman Park

Cheesman Park is a beloved Denver landmark, but for some, it's more than just a place to spend a leisurely day. The park is said to be home to the spirits of those buried there in the late 1800s.

The story of Cheesman Park is a tragic one. In the late 1800s, the area was home to a cemetery called Mount Prospect. It was the final resting place for many of the city's pioneers, but it was eventually closed due to overcrowding.

In 1890, the city of Denver purchased the land and decided to turn it into a park. To make room for the park, the remains of those buried in the cemetery were moved to other cemeteries around the city. Unfortunately, the remains of many of those buried there were not moved and were instead left in the ground when the park was built.

With the knowledge that this picturesque family park is built on a graveyard, it is not surprising that this is one of the most haunted places in Colorado. Tales of paranormal activity here actually date back to the time when the bodies were being 'removed.' One of the workmen, a man named Jim Astor, actually walked off the job after his brush with the paranormal. He had been stealing brass from the old coffins to sell for scrap when he suddenly felt an ice-cold pressure settling around his shoulders. He was convinced that one of the dead had come to reprimand him for his thievery. He was so terrified that he threw down his pilfered brass and ran from the cemetery. He never came back.

Around the same time, the people who lived in residences surrounding the graveyard began to report strange occurrences. It is said that sad and confused-looking figures would knock on their doors and windows. Many reports of disembodied moaning and crying came from the open graves in the cemetery during the exhumation work.

Today, the spirits have still not managed to find rest. There are frequent reports from visitors and the nearby residents of paranormal activity in Cheesman Park both in the daylight hours and after dark. Visitors say that they have heard the sound of hundreds of whispering voices and moans echoing around the park.

One of the common sightings in Cheesman Park involves the ghosts of little children who are often seen playing in various areas of the park in the dead of night.

However, they will disappear suddenly when people get too close.

There are so many tales of paranormal activity in Cheesman Park, and with some 2000 corpses still under the ground and thousands more graves having been desecrated, there are plenty of spirits hanging around. These forgotten souls are said to haunt the park, and visitors have reported strange sights and sounds.

There have been sightings of a woman in white wandering through the park, as well as a phantom carriage that can be heard clattering through the night. People have also reported feeling a strange presence in the park as if the souls of those buried there are still watching over them.

Harper's Ferry - Railroad

Harper's Ferry, West Virginia is a small town with a rich history of supernatural sightings. One of the most famous of these sightings is the story of the 'Ghost Girl Hit by Train,' which has been told for generations.

The legend tells that a young girl was walking along the railroad tracks late one night when she was hit by a passing train.

She was instantly killed and her ghost has been seen ever since, walking along the tracks and warning people of the danger.

The legend has been around for so long that it has become part of the local folklore. People who live in the area still tell the story, even though the incident happened decades ago.

Many people who have seen the ghost girl, report that she is wearing a white dress and possibly a white veil over her face. Some people even claim to have heard her voice, warning them to stay away from the railroad tracks.

The Legend of Octavia Hatcher

One of the saddest Appalachian ghost stories is that of Octavia Hatcher. Mrs. Hatcher had just given birth to her first child, Jacob when she came down with a mysterious illness in January of 1891. Her little boy died just a short time after being born, and locals believed that Octavia soon began suffering from depression.

The depression evolved into a coma-like state. The doctors eventually lost their battle with this disease and Octavia died on May 2, or so they believed. Within several days, many people in town began experiencing a similar illness and also drifted into a sleep-like state.

The town's doctor soon realized his mistake in the diagnosis of Octavia, and it dawned on him that she had been buried alive. The doctor ordered her body to be exhumed, and she was dug up that day. Much to their horror, those who opened the casket discovered that she had died a horrible death caused by asphyxiation. There were scratch marks in the casket lid where she had tried to escape.

Mrs. Hatcher was re-interred in the same family plot. To this day, there are stories about a misty apparition around the grave. Residents swear that they hear crying in the area near Octavia's grave site at night.

Ghosts Of The Battle Of Gettysburg

You can usually count on paranormal activity at places where the loss of life was sudden and unexpected. Then there is no wonder that a place where approximately 165,600 soldiers met, nearly 8,000 died, plus one known civilian death, and all in three days, would be considered one of the most haunted places in America. July 1 – 3, 1863 this happened all in a little town in Pennsylvania called Gettysburg.

Nearly 4 months after the battle, then President Lincoln dedicated a cemetery to the Union soldiers and in his address stated, "The world will little note, nor long remember, what we say here, but it can never forget what they did here." He was only partially right. The National Park Service took over the battlefield in 1933 and since then has done everything it can to restore the area (6,000 acres) to the conditions of 1863.

Not only has America not forgotten, but it seems some of the participants of those horrific three days have not forgotten either. Some died instantly; some were brought to make-shift hospitals in the town itself only to die later and some would be unfortunate enough to lay wounded until death found them. It is these instances that make Gettysburg a hot spot for paranormal activity.

Though the main area of paranormal activity seems to be the battlefield itself, there is also particular a spot called the Devil's Den, in the town which is also susceptible to activity. For example, countless dead were brought to the town, and in addition to that, the number of dead animals lying in the field, made the town reek of death. So, the townspeople would use lilac water to cover up the smell of death. That smell of lilac is reported to be in the air during many ghost sightings.

Many photographers as well as visitors have had their cameras malfunction in this area, photographs do not come out, apparitions in the picture, and even backgrounds of the grassy fields in the pictures come out black.

The Battle of Gettysburg was one of the most significant battles of the American Civil War, resulting in the Union victory and the turning point of the war. It was also a bloody battle, with over 50,000 casualties. It is no wonder then that it is said to be haunted by the ghosts of those who died during the battle.

The most famous ghost of Gettysburg is the "Ghost of the Angle". This is an apparition of a man, believed to be a Union soldier from the 20th Maine Infantry Regiment, which fought in the battle. The ghost has been seen many times by locals and visitors alike and is believed to be searching for his lost comrades.

Another famous ghost is the "Ghost of the High Water Mark". This ghost is said to haunt the area where the Confederate forces made their last stand. It is said that the ghost is searching for his fallen comrades and can be heard calling out their names.

There are also many other ghosts said to haunt the battlefield, including the "Ghost of the Wheatfield", which is said to be the spirit of a Confederate soldier who was killed during the battle. There are also reports of ghostly cavalrymen riding through the battlefield and of ghostly drums heard in the night.

The Battle of Gettysburg was a tragic event, and it is only natural that the spirits of those who died there still haunt the area.

Ghosts Of The Battle Of Antietam

The Battle of Antietam is one of the most important and bloodiest battles in the history of the United States. It was fought on September 17th, 1862 in Sharpsburg, Maryland, and pitted Union forces led by General George McClellan against Confederate troops led by General Robert E. Lee. The battle resulted in over 23,000 casualties and is considered the bloodiest single-day battle in American history.

The aftermath of the Battle of Antietam has left an indelible mark on the area, and it is said that the ghosts of the battle still linger in the area. Over the years, there have been numerous reports of ghostly apparitions appearing in the area, believed to be the spirits of those who fought and died in the battle.

One of the most frequently reported sightings is of a headless soldier, believed to be the ghost of a Confederate soldier whose head was blown off during the battle. Others have reported seeing a figure in a Union uniform walking along the battlefield, while others have reported seeing a ghostly figure riding a horse.

There is a story of a resident of Sharpsburg who visited the battlefield early one morning and saw several men in Confederate uniforms walking down the lane toward him. He assumed they were reenactors; the sound of his phone drew his attention from the men. On answering his cell phone, he looked up to find the soldiers had vanished.

The most famous story of Bloody Lane involves a group of boys from the McDonna School in Baltimore. The children had toured the battlefield for most of the day and ended the trip at Bloody Lane. The boys were asked to record their impressions for a history. The comments that got the most attention from the teacher were written by several boys who walked down the road to the observation tower, which is located where the Irish Brigade charged the Confederate line.

The boys described hearing strange noises that became shouts, coming from the field near the tower. Some of them said it sounded like a Christmas song in a foreign language that sounded like "Deck the Halls."

There have also been reports of strange lights in the area, believed to be the spirits of Civil War soldiers. These lights are believed to move around the battlefield and beyond and are said to create a feeling of unease or dread in those who observe them.

The ghosts of Antietam are said to be a reminder of the horror and tragedy of war. They serve as a reminder that war is not something to be taken lightly, and of the sacrifices made by those who fought and died in the Battle of Antietam. To this day, the area around the battlefield is believed to be haunted by the ghosts of those who lost their lives in one of the most significant battles in American history.

Ghosts Of Fort Delaware on Pea Patch Island

The ghosts of Fort Delaware have been a part of the local folklore since the mid-1800s when the fort was first constructed. Located on Pea Patch Island in the Delaware River, Fort Delaware was built to protect the major port of Wilmington from enemy forces during the Civil War. Over the years, many reports of ghostly activity have been reported within the fort's walls.

This harbor defense facility is now a museum that is said to be one of Delaware's most haunted places. The spirits of former Confederate soldiers who were prisoners there during the Civil War are believed to "still occupy" the facility. The soldier's ghosts have been seen by visitors on tours, and they have also appeared in photos.

Today, the paranormal activity is still strong at Fort Delaware. So many deaths in such cruel conditions have produced one of the most haunted places in America. Starting in the basement, people have claimed to hear moans, chains rattling, and voices. Apparitions of Confederate soldiers running under the ramparts have also been seen. It has been suggested that these ghosts are still looking for ways to escape the prison camp.

There is a woman apparition that visits the officer's kitchen seen by re-enactors. She has yet to be identified but she has been known to call out names and move things around. Maybe she had some form of authority in the kitchen? There have been many pictures taken at the fort and some have unexplained orbs, mists, and some even show the presence of soldiers in them.

Some of the other paranormal activity includes one of the buildings having an apparition of a woman and a child attached to it. In the building, it is said you can hear children laughing, falling objects, candles moving, and a woman crying. There have been reports by multiple people about being touched or tugged on around Fort Delaware. Claims of men swearing and a harmonica playing have been heard as well.

The most commonly reported hauntings involve a ghostly soldier who is said to patrol the fort's grounds in full uniform. Witnesses describe this ghostly figure as a tall, slim man with a stern face and a large helmet. He is often seen walking along the old stone walls of the fort or standing guard at the entrance. Some have also reported hearing the sound of drums echoing in the night air. It is believed that this phantom soldier is the spirit of a Union soldier who lost his life during the Civil War.

The Ghosts Of Mackinac Island

Mackinac Island, located off the coast of Michigan in the United States, is known for its picturesque beauty and rich history. It is also known for its haunted past and the ghosts that still haunt the island today.

The site of two major battles during the War of 1812 and a host of other violent events over the years, this picturesque island is a hotbed of paranormal activity. One notably haunted spot is the Drowning Pool, where a witch hunt was conducted in the 1700s and early 1800s. Seven women who were accused of being witches were thrown into the water with rocks tied to their feet; if they sank, they were deemed innocent.

The Ghosts of Mackinac Island have been spotted for centuries, and have become a popular tourist attraction. The most famous spirit is said to be that of Madeline, a young woman who died tragically in the 17th century. Madeline is said to haunt the Grand Hotel and is known to appear in different areas of the hotel, such as the lobby and the grounds. She is said to be in search of her lover, who was lost at sea.

Another popular spirit is that of a Native American Chief, who is said to haunt the island's forests and beaches. He is said to have died in battle, and his spirit is said to protect the island from harm.

In addition, other spirits are said to haunt Mackinac Island. There is the spirit of a young boy who was killed while swimming off the shore, and the spirit of a woman who was murdered in the island's fort.

The Ghosts of Mackinac Island have become a popular tourist attraction, and many visitors to the island have reported seeing these spirits.

Lake Huron

One of the most famous ghosts of the north-eastern United States is that of Minnie Quay, a young teenager who has been haunting the shores of Lake Huron for over a century.

Minnie Quay was the daughter of James and Mary Ann Quay, proprietors of a local Tavern in Forester Michigan built in 1852. At just 15 years of age, Minnie Quay fell victim to a sailor who came regularly into port at

Forester. Being from an upper-class family, her parents weren't very accepting of their daughter being in the company of a young seaman.

Already saddened by her parents' disapproval, Minnie Quay's heart was broken when she found out that the vessel the ship the sailor worked on sank in a storm. Sadly, she did not get a chance to say goodbye.

Driven out of her mind, Minnie made her way to the shore of Lake Huron and took her own life. She drowned herself in the lake near the family tavern in 1876.

Minnie Quay's ghost has been reported in the area for well over a century now. Her apparition is seen on the shore as if searching the high seas for her lover's ship to come ashore.

Another famous spirit of the Lake Huron ghosts is the "Grinning Man". This ghostly figure is said to appear on the lake's shoreline, often near dark, wearing a tattered hat and a grin from ear to ear. Some believe that this ghost is the spirit of a man who died in a shipwreck off the coast of Lake Huron.

Another ghostly tale is that of the "Woman in White". According to legend, this ghostly woman is the spirit of a woman who died in a drowning accident in the lake. She is said to appear on the shoreline, often wearing a white dress and carrying a lantern. Some claim that she is searching for her lost love.

The Ghost Of Emily's Bridge

Also known as Gold Brook Bridge, this site in Stowe Vermont is said to be haunted by a girl named Emily, who had arranged to meet her lover at the bridge, so they could run off and elope. When he didn't show, she hung herself from the rafters.

Visitors to the bridge have reported several strange occurrences, including seeing scratch marks appear on vehicles, hearing footsteps, and spotting a white apparition.

Haunted Forsyth Park

Forsyth Park in Savannah, Georgia has a long and storied history. Located in the center of the historic district, the park was originally established in 1851 and has been a gathering spot for Savannahians ever since. But the park is also said to be haunted by a variety of spirits, including the restless souls of Confederate soldiers who died in the Civil War.

The entire city of Savannah is pretty much one giant ghost story, due in large part to the mysterious tunnels that run below the town's streets. The underground structures play a major role in many of Savannah's most haunted locations, including Forsyth Park.

Fort Ticonderoga

Fort Ticonderoga, located in upstate New York, is a historic fort that has seen many battles and witnessed many lives lost on its grounds. As one of the oldest forts in the United States, it has a long and rich history, and it is also a place that is said to be haunted by the spirits of those who

fought in the battles that took place at the fort.
This particular stretch of land has seen countless battles.

The territory that is occupied by Fort Ticonderoga was the home of varying Native tribes. Then about 400 years ago, Samuel de Champlain discovered the terrain after a long voyage from Europe. It wasn't until 1754 that the French began constructing Fort Ticonderoga to defend what is now upstate New York, at the southern end of Lake Champlain.

The fort, completed in 1757, was detrimental to the defensive stance of the French and Native American armies as they battled with Great Britain for control of the new land.

It is not surprising with the many battles and deaths, that stories of spirits frequent this area. The most famous ghost of Fort Ticonderoga is the ghost of a British soldier who died in a battle at the fort in 1758. According to the legend, the soldier was killed by a cannonball, and his ghost has been seen roaming the grounds ever since. He is often seen in the barracks area of the fort and some believe that he is searching for his missing limb.

Other ghosts have been seen in the fort over the years, including a phantom woman in white and a spectral soldier in a red coat. There are also reports of strange noises and unexplained sightings in the fort, and some believe that these are the spirits of those who lost their lives in the battles that took place here.

Fort Ticonderoga is a popular destination for ghost hunters and paranormal enthusiasts due to its haunted history and the many sightings that have been reported over the years.

Fort Monroe

Fort Monroe, located in Hampton, Virginia, is one of the most haunted places in the United States. This former military installation has a long and rich history, and it's said that the ghosts of its former residents still linger there today.

Fort Monroe in Hampton, Va. is the largest fort in the United States. It was originally built to protect Jamestown and was used to control the coastline during the Civil War. It is one of only four Southern forts that can lay claim that it was never captured. With the long and historic role, it has played in America's past it is no wonder it is one of the most haunted places in America.

There is no wonder that due to the historical significance of this grand stone fortress some of its ghostly inhabitants are well-known participants in American history. Abraham Lincoln has been reported seen in the house called Old Quarter's Number One standing next to the fireplace. Also, reports of the great Northern General, Ulysses S. Grant have been seen around the house.

For two years, from 1885-87, Confederate President Jefferson Davis was imprisoned in the fort. His apparition has been reportedly seen walking near the flagpole of the fort. His wife, Varina, who stayed in the home across from his cell, has also been reported standing in the window of her old room staring at where Jefferson Davis was held.

Other paranormal activity reported around Fort Monroe includes that of the wife of an officer stationed at the fort. He was a very jealous man, known for his fits of rage, and much older than his wife. His wife soon fell for a younger man. Caught by the husband, he drew his pistol and shot his wife dead. His wife's spirit, known as the Luminous Lady, is said to walk the Ghost Alley behind the officer's quarters.

Another spirit associated with the alley is that of a child. Said to be in the basement of an enlisted man's home, occupants have heard a child's laugh and toys have been turned on and off and moved around. Though no history of this child has been discovered, it is said that it is around 5 years old.

Today, Fort Monroe is a popular tourist destination and is known for its ghostly activity. Visitors have reported seeing the ghosts of soldiers walking the grounds, while others have heard mysterious noises coming from the fort's old barracks. There have also been reports of a ghostly woman in white, who is believed to be the spirit of a former resident of the fort.

Perhaps one of the most famous Fort Monroe ghosts is the spirit of the fort's former commander, General Benjamin Butler. He was known for his harsh treatment of Confederate prisoners and his decision to give refuge to escaped slaves. It's said that Butler's spirit can still be seen roaming the grounds of the fort, and visitors have reported seeing him in the old parade grounds.

Sachs Bridge

Gettysburg will forever be associated with one of the bloodiest battles of the Civil War. Three days in July that permanently changed the direction of a nation. One of the places closely associated with this battle is a 100-foot-long covered bridge called Sachs.

At the beginning of the American Civil War, the Sachs Bridge was used as a focal point for the Battle of Gettysburg. Despite its historical significance, the bridge has also become known for its tales of paranormal activity and ghostly encounters.

The most famous of the Gettysburg ghosts is the "Sightless Soldier," a spectral figure who is said to appear at Sachs Bridge. Sightings of the soldier were first reported in the late 19th century and have been recounted by locals ever since. Some believe that the Sightless Soldier is the spirit of a Confederate soldier who was killed in the battle and is searching for his lost comrades.

Other tales of ghostly activity at Sachs Bridge include reports of a mysterious light that appears in the middle of the bridge at night, as well as inexplicable sounds and smells. People have also reported hearing the sound of horse hooves and the clanking of metal as if cavalry were riding across the bridge.

In addition to the Sightless Soldier, Sachs Bridge is also said to be haunted by the "Shrouded Woman," a woman dressed in a white gown who is said to appear in the early hours of the morning. Some believe that she is the spirit of a nurse who was killed during the battle and is searching for wounded soldiers.

Haunted America

CHAPTER SEVEN
HAUNTED THEATERS

Next to mausoleums and drafty old castles, it is a theatre that offers more paranormal activity than others. The theatre is an art form that has been around for centuries. It has been home to countless performances, from comedies to tragedies, and has been a source of entertainment and inspiration for countless generations. But as with any art form, there have been stories of hauntings and other supernatural occurrences in and around theatres.

No matter the location, theatre hauntings are often attributed to the same thing: the fact that theatres are places where emotions run high and memories are made. The energy of the performances and the people who occupy the space can sometimes linger long after the curtains close.

The Ghost Boy Of Albuquerque New Mexico's Kimo Theater

There's more going on behind the scenes at Albuquerque New Mexico's Kimo Theater than meets the eye. It's said that the historic theater is haunted by a little boy named Bobby, who tragically died in the theater in 1951 when a water heater in the lobby exploded.

The mysterious ghost boy has been the subject of many ghost stories over the years. The ghost is said to be a young boy of about 10 years old, wearing a white t-shirt and blue jeans. He is said to be seen roaming the theater, and many people have reported seeing him in the back row, near the projection booth.

The ghost boy has been around for over 70 years, with reports of sightings dating back to the 1950s. The ghost is believed to be harmless, and many people have reported feeling comforted by his presence. He is a popular figure in the local ghost stories, and people often tell stories of their encounters with him.

There are also many theories as to why the ghost of the Kimo Theater haunts the theater. Some believe that he is searching for his family, as he died before they could come and get him. Others think he is trying to protect the theater from any danger.

Performers and the theater's staff sometimes leave small toys and presents to distract Bobby and keep him from disrupting the show. When he's not amused, Bobby has been known to cause technical difficulties.

Ghosts Of The Dock Street Theatre

This working performance arts theater has had an eventful past, including fires and even an earthquake, since it opened in 1735. It's considered one of the most haunted places in Charleston, with two ghosts roaming the theater.

When it comes to haunted places, few locations in the United States are as haunted as the Dock Street Theatre in Charleston, South Carolina. The building, which was built in 1736, has a long and storied history filled with tales of ghosts and strange occurrences, making it one of the most haunted places in the entire South.

The theatre was originally built as a warehouse and later converted into a theatre in the early 1800s. It was the first theatre in the United States, and it is said that the building was the site of many plays, musical performances, and other events. It was also used as a gathering place for the city's elite, making it a popular destination for tourists and locals alike.

The building has a dark history that is filled with tragedy and death. In 1838, a fire broke out in the theatre and killed hundreds of people. It is said that the ghost of the tragic event still haunts the theatre to this day, with visitors reporting hearing screams and voices coming from the theatre's walls.

One of the famous ghosts is that of a young woman named Nettie Dickenson, also known as the Grey Lady. It is believed that the Grey Lady died in the theatre in 1820. Ever since her death, Nettie's ghost has been seen wandering the halls of the theatre.

There have been numerous accounts of people seeing the Grey Lady walking around the theatre. Some have described her as a slender figure wearing a long gray dress and a veil. Others have reported hearing her voice throughout the theatre or seeing a strange light in the building.

In addition to the Grey Lady, there have also been reports of other paranormal activity in the theatre. People have reported hearing strange noises and feeling a chill in the air. Many people also believe that the spirits of former actors are still lingering in the theatre, watching the performances from beyond the grave.

The most famous of all the ghosts at the Dock Street Theatre is that of a man named Junius Booth, the father of the famous actor John Wilkes Booth. Junius is said to have acted in the theatre before his son's infamous assassination of President Lincoln. His ghost is said to still haunt the theatre, and visitors have reported seeing his apparition walking the stage.

The Ghost Of The New Amsterdam Theater

The New Amsterdam Theater had a long history before it was acquired by Disney Theatrical Productions and became the home of the musical Aladdin. New Amsterdam Theatre boasts a rich history as Broadway's oldest theater and an official New York City Landmark that is also listed on the National Register of Historic Places.

Built in 1902-03, the New Amsterdam Theatre also features a resident ghost, none other than Ziegfeld Follies chorus girl and actress Olive Thomas, who was known as "The Most Beautiful Girl in New York City" before dying in Paris in 1920 at the age of 25 after swallowing a lethal dose of mercury bichloride pills (which her husband, Jack Pickford, brother of actress Mary Pickford, was used to treat his syphilis). The ghost of Thomas has often been spotted hanging out both onstage and in the backstage of the theater.

The Lincoln Theater

The Lincoln Theater was built in 1916, but the haunting history that surrounds the spectacular building goes back far beyond the theater's construction. Rumors of the Lincoln Theater being haunted began as early as the 1930s. People have felt "strange vibes", and suffered loss of breath, blackouts, and eerie feelings of being watched, touched, or even held down by an unseen force. Footsteps have been heard on the stage when there was no one else in the theater. Voices have been reported from various locations, though no one else was present to speak them.

The Capitol Theater

The Capitol Theater in Salt Lake City, Utah is one of the oldest theaters in the country and it is said to be haunted by the ghost of a former employee. The theater was built in 1919 and has been in operation for over 100 years. It is a popular destination for both locals and tourists alike, and many people have experienced strange occurrences while visiting the theater.

The reported paranormal history of the Capitol Theater seems to begin in 1947 when a teenage usher was killed when a portion of the building caught fire. The ghost of this usher, dubbed George by the workers, is said to appear from time to time.

George is a prankster – he has been known to unplug extension cords, move spotlights, and play with the locks on the many doors in the complex. There are even cases where, beneath the stage, people have become trapped between a series of two doors, which would mysteriously lock on their own.

There are also stories of electronic equipment malfunctioning inside the theater when they were in perfect working order before entering. There is also an elevator in the building that will travel from floor to floor with no passengers, with floor buttons that will light up on their own.

The area immediately surrounding the Capitol Theater, called the West Temple and 2nd South area, also has a bleak history that may contribute to the paranormal goings on in the theater. Nearby banks and hotels have all gained reputations as haunted places, with reports of ghosts and poltergeist activity.

This area of Salt Lake City was the location of the murder of the Emanuel David family, where a mother tossed her children off the 12th floor of a nearby hotel. There have also been other, more mundane murders in the area. People have also reported hearing the screams of a child, saying: "Mom, don't make me do it!"

The Royalty Theater

The Royalty Theater in Clearwater, Florida, has been the home of several ghosts for decades now, including one rather famous ghost known as "The Captain".

The Royalty Theater was built in the 1920s by John S. Taylor, Senator-elect. Construction began in 1920 but was damaged by a storm and reconstructed as the New Capitol Theater. In the 1930s, the haunted theater promoted vaudevillian shows every Friday night. Managed by multiple movie companies over the years, the next few decades went great for the theater. Renovations in 1962 kept the movie house up to date and brought in bigger crowds.

Things weren't going so well in the 1970's, however, and Pitt Southern – the theater's managing company at that time – chose not to renew its contract in 1979. The establishment was forced to close its doors in 1980.

Just one year later, the theater was re-opened and rebranded The Royalty Theater. Everything was looking up until the body of Bill Neville was found in the balcony area. He had been robbed and murdered during renovations; some say because he was believed to be homosexual.

Bill is just one of the ghosts suspected of haunting the Royalty Theater. Footsteps have been heard on the balcony when no one is there. Another ghost to frequent the Royalty Theater is that of a small girl, estimated to be about

9 to 12 years old. She has appeared at random to various guests and staff members and is kind of known as a guardian of the theater.

The main attraction for paranormal activists is the Captain. He has been haunting the Royalty Theater for decades and has been sighted countless times throughout the building. His name comes from his clothing. The Captain sports a fisherman's hat, blue coat, blue eyes, and a goatee.

There are many reports of the lights, especially the ones backstage, turning on and off by themselves. The alarms have been known to go off when no one was near close enough to trigger them. Orbs and "mists" have appeared in many pictures taken in the theater. The chandelier has started swinging noticeably during and after shows.

One of the most interesting stories of the Royalty Theater haunting is a knife-like shape that appears on one of the stage walls. Coat after coat of paint, more than 20 in all, and the strange silhouette remains.

Some people believe that the ghosts at the Royalty Theater are harmless, while others believe that they can be mischievous. However, there have been no reports of the ghosts ever harming anyone.

Barter Theater

The Barter Theater in Abington, Virginia is believed to be haunted by numerous otherworldly specters, but primarily by the ghost of its founder, Robert Portfield. His love for the theater was well known and after spending nearly 40 years within its walls, it's little surprise he chose to stay there after his demise.

The Barter Theatre in Abington, Virginia, is one of the oldest and most respected professional theaters in the United States. It is also said to be one of the most haunted theaters in the country.

The theater was founded in 1933 during the Great Depression, and it quickly became a popular destination for people from all over the country. The theater was known for its high-quality productions and its affordable prices.

During the early years of the theater, several deaths occurred on the property. The most famous death was that of Robert Porterfield, the founder of the theater. Porterfield died in 1976, but he is said to still roam the theater to this day.

Another ghost that is said to haunt the Barter Theatre is that of a young actress who died in a car accident while on her way to a performance. Her ghost is said to still roam the theater, and she has been seen and heard by many people.

There have been numerous reports of paranormal activity at the Barter Theatre, including people seeing or hearing the ghosts of Robert Porterfield and the young actress, objects moving on their own, doors opening/closing on their own, cold spots, and electronic equipment malfunctioning.

Calumet Theater

The Calumet Theatre in Calumet, Michigan, is a historic theater that is said to be haunted by several ghosts. The most famous ghost is that of Madame Helena Modjeska, a renowned Polish actress who died in 1909. She is said to have performed at the Calumet Theatre on several occasions, and her ghost is often seen wandering the theater's halls.

Another ghost that is said to haunt the Calumet Theatre is that of a young girl named Elanda Rowe. Rowe died in a mysterious fire at the theater in 1893, her ghost is said to be seen and heard in the theater to this day.

There have been numerous reports of paranormal activity at the Calumet Theatre, including people seeing or hearing the ghosts of Madame Helena Modjeska and Elanda Rowe, objects moving on their own, doors opening and closing on their own, cold spots being felt, and electronic equipment malfunctioning.

The Lyric Theater in Alabama

One night, a group of actors were rehearsing for a play in the theater. They were the only ones in the building, and they were all downstairs in the rehearsal room. Suddenly, they heard the sound of footsteps coming from upstairs. They thought it was the janitor, but when they went to investigate, they found that the upstairs was empty.

The actors went back to rehearsing, but the footsteps continued. They started to get scared, and they eventually decided to leave the theater. As they were walking out, they saw a shadowy figure standing in the doorway. The figure waved to them, and then it disappeared.

The actors were terrified, and they refused to go back to the theater for several days. When they finally did go back, they were very careful to stay together and to avoid being alone in the theater.

The Lyric Theatre in Birmingham, Alabama is said to be haunted by several ghosts:

A former stage manager named Antoine. He is often seen or heard moving things around the theater, and he is even said to have hummed or sung to people.

A former usher named Mary. She is often seen on the stairs or in the aisles of the theater, and she is said to be very friendly and welcoming to visitors.

A former performer named George. He is often seen or heard singing or dancing on the stage, and he is said to be very playful and mischievous.

There have been numerous reports of paranormal activity at the Lyric Theatre, including people seeing or hearing the ghosts of Antoine, Mary, or George. objects moving on their own, doors opening/closing on their own, cold spots being felt, and electronic equipment malfunctioning.

Old Tampa Theatre

The Old Tampa Theatre is situated in the very heart of the city. Considered America's most richly ornate theatrical "palace", it has been running for nearly a century now, and is said to be haunted by several ghosts who manifest themselves within its walls.

The story dates back to 1930 when Foster "Fink" Finley was hired to run the projector at Old Tampa Theatre. He remained under its employment until a fatal heart attack in 1965. It is said that Fink was so devoted to his job that he showed up several hours early for work every day. After 35 years of dedication, it's no surprise that the ghost of Fink would haunt the theatre today.

His spirit is said to manifest in several ways, including a human-shaped shadow that will cast itself across the movie screen during a film. Strange noises are said to come from the projector booth when no one is in there. Doors have been reported opening and closing when no one is in the area to shift them.

Fink's ghost is also thought to pull pranks on other staff members of the theatre. Several times employees have claimed that when trying to close the door to the projection room, it seems as if someone is holding it open for a moment before they can close it.

Other ghosts of Old Tampa Theatre include:

A 'White Lady' who has been seen on the balcony of the theatre.

An apparition described as wearing light clothing appears in the theatre seats as if watching a production when the theatre is closed.

A dapper, mysterious ghost known only as "fedora man." He is often seen sitting in seat 308, wearing a suit and a fedora hat. Some people believe that he is the spirit of a former theater patron, while others believe that he is a guardian spirit who watches over the theater.

Haunted America

CHAPTER EIGHT
HAUNTED CEMETERIES

Haunted Cemeteries always bring about mental imagery of creepy settings and feelings of uneasiness. When people think of haunted locations, cemeteries are probably second to haunted houses. But why would a ghost want to hang around a cemetery? The locations are pretty lifeless.

Wouldn't a ghost choose a place filled with life and memories? A cemetery is a place of eternal rest. But what happens when these peaceful places become shrouded in mystery? Haunted cemeteries are said to be home to spirits, poltergeists, and other supernatural entities. Some people claim to have seen ghosts walking among the headstones, while others have heard eerie noises coming from the graveyard at night.

There are many stories about haunted cemeteries. Some of them are based on actual events. In the United States, several cemeteries are documented by paranormal investigators. These places are often the setting for some of the most memorable stories.

The Cemetery That Became Lincoln Park Zoo

Lions, and tigers, and...ghosts? Yes, one of Chicago's most popular attractions is also one of its most haunted, with much more than just wildlife roaming the grounds.

Lincoln Park Zoo in Chicago, Illinois was built on the site of a former cemetery. The cemetery was in use from 1843 to 1866, and it is estimated that over 35,000 people were buried there. When the cemetery was closed, many of the bodies were exhumed and moved. It was said the cemetery closed, due to its proximity to the city's water supply, and most of the bodies—but not all of them. Yes, most of the bodies, were moved.

If you watched the movie *Poltergeist*, then you know the dead don't like their rest disturbed. Messing with burial grounds is the easiest way to get haunted, and the Lincoln Park Zoo is no exception. People have reported seeing ghosts there since it opened 150 years ago.

Over the years, there have been many reports of paranormal activity at the zoo. Visitors have reported seeing ghosts of people who were buried in the cemetery, hearing disembodied voices, and feeling cold spots.

Some of the most common ghost sightings at the zoo include:

A woman dressed in white walking through the zoo at night.

A man standing in the shadow of the lion's house.

Children playing in the zoo's playground.

In addition to ghost sightings, there have also been reports of other paranormal activity at the zoo, such as objects moving on their own, doors opening/closing on their own, strange noises such as whispers and footsteps, cold spots, and electrical equipment malfunctioning.

Some people believe that the ghosts at Lincoln Park Zoo are harmless, while others believe that they can be mischievous or even malevolent. However, there have been no reports of the ghosts ever harming anyone.

Violin Annie St. Louis, IL Elmwood Cemetery

She died at the age of 11 of diphtheria and legend has it that if you enter the cemetery at night, you can hear the sounds of Annie playing her violin ever so softly. In life, she loved her violin and played it for family and friends daily. She was so attached to her violin that after her death the family had a massive monument of her holding her violin erected for her.

There have been many reports of people hearing Violin Annie play her violin over the years. Some people have even claimed to see her ghost standing next to her grave, playing her violin.

Violin Annie is one of the most famous ghosts in Illinois, and her ghost is said to be very active at Elmwood Cemetery.

Greenwood Cemetery

Greenwood Cemetery in Decatur, Illinois is one of the most well-documented haunted places, with hundreds of reports of paranormal activity over the years.

The cemetery is home to the ghosts of many people, including Civil War soldiers, Confederate prisoners, and children who died in a flood. It can be verified that the dates of burials go back to 1840, but no one knows how long this area has been used as a burial ground.

There are some indications that Native Americans used a part of the current cemetery, as sacred burial grounds. There is possible evidence of that in unmarked graves towards the southern tip of the cemetery. Though it is not clear as to when the cemetery was first being used, it is clear, that by 1920 it was falling into a state of disrepair.

By the 1950's, Greenwood cemetery lay in ruins. It was around this time that the ghost stories started being told. There was a flood during this period that moved some of the graves. The bodies were relocated to another part of the cemetery; and reburied. Since then, there have been strange balls of light, hovering over the original area of the graves.

There are many stories of paranormal activity at Greenwood Cemetery. Probably the most noted is the appearance of the spirit known as the Greenwood Bride. In the 1930's there was a young couple who was getting ready to elope. The young man was killed that night and thrown into the river. He was later buried somewhere in the cemetery. Upon finding out about the death of her boyfriend, the girl took her own life the following day in the same river.

Though her parents never approved of the wedding, they found the bridal gown and thought it to be an appropriate dress for their daughter to be buried in. There have been several eyewitness accounts of seeing a young girl in a bridal dress walking around looking at headstones. She is said to be always crying.

Some of the most famous ghosts at Greenwood Cemetery include:

The Civil War Soldier: A ghostly soldier is often seen walking through the cemetery, wearing a Union uniform and carrying a rifle. He is believed to be the spirit of a soldier who was killed in the Civil War and buried in the cemetery.

The Confederate Prisoners: A group of Confederate prisoners are said to haunt the cemetery. They are believed to be the spirits of prisoners who died while being transported to a prison camp during the Civil War.

The Children: A group of children are said to haunt the cemetery. They are believed to be the spirits of children who died in a flood in the late 1800s.

In addition to these famous ghosts, many other ghosts are said to haunt Greenwood Cemetery. Visitors have reported seeing ghosts of people who were buried in the cemetery, hearing disembodied voices, and feeling cold spots. Some people have even claimed to be touched or shoved by ghosts.

Resurrection Mary

So much rich history can be found in Chicago. Al Capone was found guilty there in 1931; John Dillinger was shot by the FBI there in 1934; home of the Comiskey Park, Wrigley Field, and Da' Bears. One of the most famous residents of the Windy City though may not have been so well known while alive, but in death has become one of the most famous ghosts in Chicago, Resurrection Mary.

Mary was a young Polish girl, around 20 years old, who was out dancing at one of the local ballrooms. One cold winter night in 1934, she was with her date at the O. Henry Ballroom, now the Willowbrook on Archer Avenue in Justice Illinois, a southern suburb of Chicago.

The very attractive blonde-haired girl got into an argument with the boy. She walked out of the ballroom, determined that she would rather walk home alone than ride home with her date. She didn't walk very far up Archer Avenue before a car skidded out of control and struck her. The driver fled the scene, leaving Mary near death on the side of the cold dark road. She was already dead by the time she was found. She was buried shortly afterward in

Resurrection Cemetery, in her white dress and dancing shoes.

Several years later, drivers along Archer Avenue started reporting strange encounters with a young woman in a white dress. She always appeared to be a real person, until she would inexplicably vanish. Some even said that their car passed directly through the girl. At that point, she would turn and disappear through the cemetery gates.

There have been sightings of Mary from the 1920s up till the present day. Policemen and cab drivers offer stories of giving rides to her, people see her standing at the entrance to the cemetery and she is apt to throw herself in front of oncoming traffic, especially young men driving alone.

The strange encounters began to move further away from the graveyard and closer to the Ballroom. She was now being reported on the nearby roadway and sometimes, inside of the ballroom itself. On many occasions, young men would meet a girl at the ballroom, dance with her, and then offer her a ride home at the end of the evening. She would always accept and offer vague directions that would lead north on Archer Avenue. When the car would reach the gates of Resurrection Cemetery, the young woman would always vanish.

One very interesting paranormal event happened in 1977. Someone saw a woman locked inside the fence of Resurrection Cemetery after dark. The passerby didn't stop, however, but instead called the police to come and assist her. The police found no one in sight when they arrived, but did find that the two bars on the main gate had been bent as if someone was pushing on them.

On the bent bars, were imprints of what looked like human hands burnt into the metal. The bars were removed by officials but later reinstalled. They tried to remove the handprints with a blowtorch, but the burns could still be seen.

What has made Resurrection Mary an interesting phenomenon is the number of people from various walks of life who have seen this apparition. From cab rides to dance halls, this apparition seems to still be living a fascinating life.

White Lady Of Bachelor's Grove

If you are seeking a place that has been claimed by the occult, and abandoned since the 1960s, then perhaps you should visit the Bachelors Grove Cemetery in Illinois. It has been said that the events that have been known to occur at the cemetery, occur because of the various groups of people that have performed occult and satanic rituals at the cemetery, which is home to overturned gravestones and over one hundred accounts of strange occurrences happening in the cemetery and the surrounding areas.

Bachelor's Grove is one of the few cemeteries with a clearly photographed ghostly image. A photograph taken there appeared in both the Chicago Sun-Times and the National Examiner. It was taken during an investigation in Bachelor's Grove Cemetery on August 10, 1991. It clearly shows a young woman sitting on a tombstone, with parts of her lower and upper body being somewhat transparent. Her clothes are also out-of-date for the period when the photo was taken.

This spirit is known as the "White Lady" or the "Madonna of Bachelor's Grove". She is said to be the ghost of a woman buried in the cemetery next to her young son.

The burial ground is said to be infested with ghosts, and more than 100 different reports, of strange phenomena have been made about the cemetery, including actual apparitions, unexplained sights and sounds, and glowing orbs of light. The ghosts range from the image of people dressed in monk's robes to the spirit of a glowing yellow man, seen in 1984. Many of these ghosts have been captured on film.

Visitors to the cemetery have experienced an eerie aura that comes with walking through the rows of broken tombstones and dug-up graves. These cemetery markers and gravestones have been known to move about on their own.

The lake that is located adjacent to the cemetery has been said to have a glowing aura at night. The algae that coats the top of the lake seems to hide everything that is said to be under the water! Apparently, in the sixties there were bodies dumped into the algae-covered lake by the mafia, looking for a place to hide the bodies of those that betrayed them. The water has also been the site of many apparitions that claim to pull a horse and carriage into the water.

Garden of Hope Cemetery

Named as one of the top 10 haunted cemeteries in the United States on many lists, The Garden of Hope Cemetery in Gautier Mississippi has more than its fair share of unusual stories that go with the graves that are there. One of the most famous stories comes with the story of a father who was meeting his wife and five children in a hotel one night for a weekend. They were going to take his much-anticipated bonus and put it on a house that they had been dreaming of for many years. However, little did any of them know, the father was going to be fired that day.

On the way to the hotel, the father kept hearing voices inside his head, telling him what needed to be done. Now was this his psychosomatic way of dealing with the loss of the dream home or was he being possessed by demons? When he got to the hotel, he greeted his family, which consisted of his wife and 5 children (aged from 6 months to 8 years old). The family knew nothing about the layoff and thought that all well good and well in their world. As the family lay sleeping and the father pretended to sleep, he kept being told by the voices what needed to be done as he was no longer able to provide for his family.

Once he knew that they were all asleep, he left the hotel and in a frenzied state, returned with a fire axe and proceeded to mutilate his entire family one by one. He then left the hotel and swinging his ax wildly in the rain walked out onto the highway and was struck dead by a truck that was carrying a propeller for a ship at the place where he was just fired from. Coincidence or Fate?

Some passersby have seen children playing among the gravestones at the Garden of Hope Cemetery, and they believe that they are the children who were murdered that night back in the late 1970s. There are tales of a man who will climb from his grave to search the neighboring grave plots for flowers to take back to his gravestone.

Another ghost said to linger at this cemetery is called "Bloody Sarah", she is seen wearing a bloody housecoat and fluffy slippers, and she is seen most often during the day running out in front of cars on the road. She is then heard laughing hysterically when they stop and get out of their vehicles because they think they hit a real person.

There have been many reports of paranormal activity at the Garden of Hope Cemetery over the years. Visitors have reported seeing the ghosts of Cheryl Anne, Hal, and Bloody Sarah, as well as hearing disembodied voices and feeling cold spots. Some people have even claimed to have been touched or pushed by the ghosts.

Union Cemetery

There have been many reports of paranormal activity at the 400-year-old Union Cemetery over the years. Visitors have reported seeing the ghosts of the White Lady, the Red Eyes, and the soldiers, as well as hearing disembodied voices and feeling cold spots. Some people have even claimed to have been touched or pushed by the ghosts.

An apparition dubbed "The White Lady" is Union Cemetery's most famous haunt. Wearing a white nightgown and a bonnet over her dark hair, the White Lady is said to walk the roads between Union Cemetery and Stepney Cemetery, 10 miles away. She is said to appear in the middle of the road, stretching her arms out to the approaching driver. Her appearance doesn't leave the driver any time to stop or swerve away, and she is invariably struck and immediately disappears, leaving no damage done to the vehicle.

There is one exception to this formula on record, however. In 1993 an off-duty fireman was traveling the road between the two cemeteries in his pickup truck when he saw the pavement in front of him glow with a red light. He then noticed that the ghost of an old farmer wearing a straw hat was sitting in the passenger seat while the White Lady appeared in the road ahead. She was struck with a thump, and then she and the mysterious passenger disappeared, leaving a dent in the front of the truck as a reminder of their visit. This is the only reported case in the area of the White Lady manifesting in conjunction with another spirit.

Another famous resident of Union Cemetery is a ghost that locals call "Red Eyes". This haunt involves visitors to the cemetery seeing a pair of glowing red eyes in the brush at the periphery of their vision, and hearing subsequent footfalls behind them as they walk away. Some paranormal investigators in the area speculate that this specter may be one Earle Kellogg, who was set on fire and killed just outside the property in 1935, while others say that it might be a drunk driver who was killed.

Union Cemetery was immortalized by paranormal experts Ed and Lorraine Warren in their book Graveyard, which includes a large amount of research about the area. The Warrens also compiled a lot of video and photographic evidence of the paranormal at Union Cemetery, including a video recording of the manifestation of the White Lady.

West Middlebury Cemetery

West Middlebury Cemetery in West Middlebury, New York was built in the early 1700s. It is a small place, with only around 100 plots, and a high concentration of spirit energy that shows up as orbs, rods, and webs in photographs.

There have been many reports of paranormal activity at West Middlebury Cemetery over the years. Visitors have reported seeing the ghosts of the Egyptian Mummy, the White Lady, the Black Dog, and the Soldier, as well as hearing disembodied voices and feeling cold spots. Some people have even claimed to have been touched or pushed by the ghosts.

West Middlebury Cemetery is said to be haunted by several ghosts, including:

The Egyptian Mummy: In 1945, the mummy of an Egyptian prince named Amum-Her-Khepesh-Ef was buried in West Middlebury Cemetery. His mummy is said to haunt the cemetery, and people have reported seeing him walking around the cemetery at night.

The White Lady: The White Lady is a ghost who is said to haunt the cemetery at night. She is often seen wearing a long white dress and carrying a bouquet of white flowers. Some people believe that she is the ghost of a bride who died on her wedding day, while others believe that she is the ghost of a young woman who was murdered in the cemetery.

The Black Dog: The Black Dog is a ghostly dog that is said to haunt the cemetery at night. He is often seen chasing people through the cemetery, and he is said to be a bad omen.

The Soldier: The Soldier is a ghost who is said to haunt the cemetery at night. He is often seen wearing a Union uniform and carrying a rifle. Some people believe that he is the ghost of a soldier who died in the Civil War, while others believe that he is the ghost of a soldier who was murdered in the cemetery.

Saint Louis Cemetery No. 1

Saint Louis Cemetery No. 1 in New Orleans, Louisiana, is one of the oldest and most famous cemeteries in the United States. It is also one of the most haunted cemeteries in the country.

The cemetery is the final resting place of many famous people, including Marie Laveau, the Voodoo Queen of New Orleans. The cemetery is also home to the tombs of many wealthy and powerful families from New Orleans' history.

There have been many reports of paranormal activity at Saint Louis Cemetery No. 1 over the years. Visitors have reported seeing ghosts walking through the cemetery, hearing disembodied voices, and feeling cold spots. Some people have even claimed to have been touched or pushed by a ghost

Built in 1789, St. Louis Cemetery No. 1, is the oldest cemetery in New Orleans. In 1975 it was listed in the

National Register of Historic Places. New Orleans is unique in that the city is below sea level. This uniqueness makes it nearly impossible to bury loved ones below ground, thus the dead are buried in vaults and mausoleums. The cemeteries which house these tombs and mausoleums have been turned into eerily beautiful works of art.

Due to the lack of land and the having to bury their dead above ground; New Orleans has an unusual way to deal with the space restrictions. Family members are placed in wooden coffins and buried in vaults for one year and a day. After that time frame, the coffin is removed and the bones of the deceased are put in a bag. The bag is then pushed to the back, leaving room for the next body.

There are a few though that would like to remain and have chosen to walk the cemetery at night. One of the most famous is Marie Laveau, Voodoo Priestess. Marie was a free Creole woman who became a hairdresser to the upper class. She began to practice Voodoo and soon garnered a huge following.

Marie Laveau died in 1881, but even today many believers leave offerings at her grave, in hopes she will bless them from the other side. Many leave three Xs on her tomb, as they make a wish in hopes she will grant it. Visitors have reported seeing her walking through the cemetery at night, wearing a long black dress and carrying a snake.

Another famous ghost at Saint Louis Cemetery No. 1 is the ghost of a little girl named Emily. Emily is said to have died in a fire at her home in the early 1900s. Her ghost is often seen playing in the cemetery or sitting on her tombstone.

Some people believe that Emily is waiting for her parents to come and pick her up, while others believe that she is simply trying to find peace.

Another spirit that has been seen is that of Henry Vignes. Henry seems to be looking for his proper burial place and has been claimed to stop people and ask if they know where his vault is. He is described as a tall man in a white shirt and has even been claimed to touch people politely on the shoulder and inquire about any information they have about a particular tomb.

Savannah Georgia's First Burial Ground

Savannah's First Burial Ground is the oldest public cemetery in the city, and it is also one of the most haunted. The cemetery was founded in 1733, and it is estimated that over 20,000 people are buried there.

There have been many reports of paranormal there over the years. Visitors have reported seeing ghosts walking through the cemetery, hearing disembodied voices, and feeling cold spots. Some people have even claimed to have been touched or pushed by ghosts.

One of the most famous ghosts at Savannah's First Burial Ground is the ghost of Rene Rondolier. Rondolier was a French soldier who was convicted of murder and hanged in the cemetery in 1816. His ghost is often seen hanging from the tree where he was executed, or walking through the cemetery at night, dragging a chain behind him.

Another famous ghost is that of a young woman named Mary Musgrove. Mary was the daughter of a Yamacraw Indian chief and an English trader. She is said to have died in childbirth in 1737, and her ghost is often seen walking through the cemetery at night, carrying her baby in her arms.

Many other ghosts haunt the cemetery including the ghosts of soldiers who died in the Revolutionary War, sailors who died in the Civil War, and victims of yellow fever outbreaks.

Savannah's First Burial Ground is a fascinating and eerie place to visit. It is a beautiful and historic cemetery that is full of mystery and intrigue.

Hollywood Cemetery

Hollywood Cemetery in Richmond, Virginia, is one of the oldest and most historic cemeteries in the United States. It is also one of the most haunted cemeteries in the country.

The cemetery is the final resting place of many famous people, including two U.S. presidents, James Monroe and John Tyler, as well as Jefferson Davis. There are also novelist Ellen Glasgow and Historians Clifford Dowdy and David J. Mays. George Pickett, J.E.B. Stuart, and Fitzhugh Lee also are there along with six Virginia governors, two Supreme Court justices, twenty-three more Confederate generals, and thousands of Confederate soldiers. Hollywood Cemetery is also the site of many historical events, including the Battle of the Crater during the Civil War.

There have been many reports of paranormal activity at Hollywood Cemetery over the years. Visitors have reported seeing ghosts of soldiers walking through the cemetery, hearing disembodied voices, and feeling cold spots. Some people have even claimed to have been touched or pushed by ghosts.

There are claims from visitors from early morning as well as the dark of night, that they hear soft moans coming from around and inside the stone pyramid monument on the grounds. Some say it is the spirits of soldiers that have not ever been identified trying to make their presence known. There are also cold spots that have been reported around one corner of the pyramid.

A little behind the pyramid is a 3-foot-high cast iron dog that has been placed by a little grave. The grave belongs to a girl who passed aware of Scarlet Fever in 1862 at the age of three. There have been many reports of a dog barking and howling near the area in the dead of night.

Another famous ghost at Hollywood Cemetery is that of a Confederate soldier named William. William is said to have been killed in the Battle of the Crater, and his ghost is often seen walking through the cemetery at night, carrying a rifle.

Many other ghosts are said to haunt Hollywood Cemetery, including the ghosts of children who died in disease outbreaks, victims of murder, and even pets.

Haunted America

CHAPTER NINE
HAUNTED CHURCHES

There are many beautiful and famous churches all over the world that tourists come to visit because of their storied history, beautiful stained glass, and architecture. But churches can also be less than holy and carry dark a history.

For as long as humans have practiced religious traditions, they have constructed buildings to gather, pray, and practice their faith. And sometimes, it's not just the living who linger in the sacred halls. Sometimes the dead still walk the grounds of these holy sites.

Restless Ghosts Of The San Fernando Cathedral

The San Fernando Cathedral in San Antonio, Texas is one of the oldest and most haunted churches in the United States. It is believed that the ghosts of many people who died in the church or on its grounds still roam the halls.

When construction workers started renovating the church in 1936, they unearthed bones, nails, and tattered military uniforms near the altar, which some believe belonged to three soldiers of the Alamo.

Since the disturbing incident, visitors have reported shadowy figures and orbs in their photographs, as well as ghosts in the back of the church itself. Such otherworldly spirits include a man dressed in black and figures in hooded, monk-like clothing.

One of the most famous ghosts at the cathedral is the ghost of a Spanish soldier who was killed in a battle against the Native Americans in the 18th century. His ghost is said to be seen walking around the cathedral at night, still wearing his uniform and carrying his weapon.

Another famous ghost at the cathedral is the ghost of a young woman who died in childbirth in the 19th century. Her ghost is said to be seen crying and wailing in the church at night, searching for her lost child.

Visitors have also reported seeing ghosts of priests, nuns, children, and even pets. Some people have even claimed to have been touched by ghosts.

Egg Hill Church

Egg Hill Church in Spring Hills, Pennsylvania is said to be haunted by the ghost of its former pastor, Reverend John B. Matthias. Matthias was a charismatic and popular preacher, but he was also known for his eccentric and sometimes disturbing behavior. In 1889, Matthias murdered his entire congregation, poisoning them with communion wine. He then hung himself in the church basement.

Matthias's ghost is said to haunt the church grounds, particularly the basement where he hanged himself. Visitors have reported seeing his ghost walking through the church, hearing his voice, and feeling cold spots. Some people have even claimed to have been touched by his ghost.

In addition to Matthias's ghost, other ghosts are said to haunt the church. Visitors have reported seeing the ghosts of the children who were murdered by Matthias, as well as the ghosts of other people, who have died on the church grounds over the years.

People have also reported hearing the cries of child victims who died at the hands of the pastor, even though the building remains locked and empty.

The Ghosts of St. Louis Cathedral

The St. Louis Cathedral in New Orleans, Louisiana is one of the oldest and most iconic cathedrals in the United States. It is also rumored to have its fair share of hauntings.

Many stories of ghosts are said to haunt the cathedral, but the most famous ghost is the ghost of Père Antoine. Père Antoine was a French priest who served at the cathedral in the late 18th century. He was a popular and beloved priest, but he was also a controversial figure. He was known for his outspokenness and his criticism of the Spanish government, which ruled Louisiana at the time.

In 1788, Père Antoine was arrested by the Spanish government and charged with treason. He was imprisoned in the cathedral for several months before being deported to France. However, Père Antoine never made it to France. He died at sea on the way, and his body was lost at sea.

Père Antoine's ghost is said to haunt the cathedral grounds, particularly the area around the altar. Visitors have reported seeing his ghost walking through the cathedral, hearing his voice, and feeling cold spots.

St. Mary's Catholic Church

There are three ghosts rumored to haunt St. Mary's Church and its grounds. One story holds that a priest died during the construction of the church. Another story claims that, during the Civil War, a Catholic priest serving as a chaplain for the Confederate Army was shot and died in the church.

There is another rumor that the ghost is the spirit of Bishop Richard Pius Miles, the first bishop of the Diocese of Nashville, who died in 1860. He was buried in the church basement and supposedly still haunts his old stomping grounds.

According to one story from 1937, a pounding at his bedroom door woke up a priest in the rectory, but he could find no one there. After he fell asleep, he was woken again, this time by a pounding on the headboard of his bed. There was no one in the room, so the awakening was attributed to supernatural causes by superstitious locals.

There have been numerous reports of strange noises, muffled figures, and apparitions at the church. Some people have claimed to have heard the sound of footsteps in empty rooms. Some visitors have also reported feeling cold spots and being touched by unseen hands.

The church is also said to be haunted by the ghost of a Confederate chaplain who was shot and killed during the Civil War. The chaplain was reportedly trying to help wounded soldiers when he was shot by a Union soldier. His ghost is said to haunt the church basement, where he was buried.

Westminster Hall

Built in 1852, this burial ground contains such famous people as Edgar Allan Poe and General James McHenry. The building is surrounded by burial grounds and catacombs which are also built over many of the graves. There have been reports of voices and apparitions being encountered. It may be a beautiful, historical location during the daylight hours, but after dark things seem to come alive.

Westminster Hall and Burying Ground in Baltimore, Maryland is rumored to be haunted by many ghosts, including:

Edgar Allan Poe: Poe is one of the most famous ghosts associated with Westminster Hall. He was buried in the burying ground in 1849, and his grave is one of the most visited in the cemetery. Some people believe that Poe's ghost haunts the cemetery, especially on his birthday and on the anniversary of his death.

Lucia Watson Taylor: Taylor was a young woman who died in 1816 at the age of 16. She is buried in the burying ground, and her grave is often visited by people who have lost loved ones. Some people believe that Taylor's ghost haunts the cemetery, and she is often seen as a misty figure dressed in white kneeling in prayer by her own grave.

The Skull of Cambridge: This is the nickname of an unknown man who was buried in the burying ground in 1777. The man's skull was said to be so large and heavy that it had to be buried in a separate box. Some people believe that the Skull of Cambridge haunts the cemetery, and it is rumored that his screams can be heard at night.

The Catacombs: The catacombs are a series of underground tunnels that were used to bury the dead in the 19th century. Some people believe that the catacombs are haunted by the ghosts of the people who are buried there.

Aquia Episcopal Church

Aquia Episcopal Church in Stafford, Virginia is rumored to be haunted by the ghost of a young woman named Blond Beth. According to legend, Beth was murdered in the church in the 18th century. Her body was not discovered until many years later when the church reopened after the Revolutionary War.

Beth's ghost is said to be seen wandering the church grounds, especially at night. She is often seen wearing a white dress and has long, blonde hair. Some people have also reported hearing her footsteps and her voice.

Many over the years have been said to have witnessed the paranormal activity. There have been reports of eerie lights and sounds from the tower, footsteps, and ghosts being seen.

In addition to the young murdered girl, there is also the story of a young man who was dared to enter the church at night and walk to the belfry alone. He was given a hammer and nail, which he was to place on the wall as proof he made it, but when he never came back, they began to worry. The next morning, his body was found nailed to the wall. Members of the church do not believe the story.

St. Olaf Kirke (Old Rock Church)

This church, built in 1886, is in the middle of Cranfills Gap, Texas. The Norwegian Church is still used by the surrounding communities and is open daily for visitors to enjoy. However, it is also listed as one of the most haunted places in Texas. It is said that in the middle of the night, past parishioners can be heard singing hymns and organs playing. There have also been apparitions seen walking in the cemetery. to see it.

St. Olaf is rumored to be haunted by many ghosts, including:

The Norwegian Settlers: The church was built in 1886 by Norwegian settlers, and some people believe that their spirits still haunt the church. Visitors have reported seeing apparitions of Norwegian settlers dressed in traditional clothing and hearing them speaking Norwegian.

The White Lady: Some people have claimed to see the ghost of a woman in white wandering the church grounds. The identity of this woman is unknown, but some people believe that she may be the ghost of a bride who was jilted at the altar or a woman who died in childbirth.

The Organist: Some people have reported hearing the sound of an organ playing in the church, even though there is no organist present. It is believed that this may be the ghost of the church's former organist, who died many years ago.

Auburn University Chapel

The Auburn University Chapel in Auburn, Alabama is rumored to be haunted by the ghost of a Confederate soldier named Sidney Grimlett. Grimlett was wounded in the Civil War and was brought to the chapel, which was serving as a hospital at the time. He died from his wounds, but his spirit is said to have remained.

Visitors to the chapel have reported seeing Grimlett's ghost, hearing his footsteps, and feeling his presence. He is often seen wearing a Confederate uniform and carrying a gun. Some people have also claimed to have been touched or pushed by Grimlett's ghost.

There are several stories about Grimlett's ghost. One story says that he is haunted by the memory of his death and is unable to move on. Another story says that he is protecting the chapel from desecration.

Haunted America

CHAPTER TEN
HAUNTED SCHOOLS

A school is a place of learning, friendships, and growth. But sometimes, schools can be places of fear and terror. Many schools across the globe have been reported to be haunted by ghosts, and these reports have been backed up by hundreds of accounts from students, teachers, and other staff members.

Haunted schools are usually quite old, often having been built hundreds of years ago. They have been the site of many strange occurrences, from the sound of eerie laughter to dark shadows moving in the hallways. Some have even reported feeling a presence in the classrooms or hearing voices coming from the walls.

Hell House (St. Mary's College)

St. Mary's College, also known as Hell House, is a former Catholic seminary in Ellicott City, Maryland, that is rumored to be haunted. The college was founded in 1851 and closed in 1968. The buildings have been abandoned since then, and the property has become overgrown with trees and brush.

The rumors of hauntings at St. Mary's College began in the 1970s. Visitors to the property have reported seeing apparitions of former students and priests, hearing strange noises, and feeling cold spots. Some people have even claimed to have been touched or pushed by unseen forces.

One of the most popular ghost stories at St. Mary's College is the story of the "White Lady." The White Lady is said to be the ghost of a young woman who died in the college's chapel. She is said to be seen wandering the grounds at night, dressed in a white dress.

Another popular ghost story is the story of the "Hanging Priest." The Hanging Priest is said to be the ghost of a priest who hanged himself in the college's bell tower.

He is said to be seen hanging from the bell tower on stormy nights.

Hibbing High School

About an hour and a half northwest of Duluth Minnesota is the town of Hibbing Minnesota. In its luxurious high school is an auditorium that has captured the attention of many ghost hunters. Built to resemble the Capitol Theater in New York City, this auditorium boasts many of the elegant. It seats 1800 but there is one seat, J47 that is occupied by the ghost of Hibbing High School.

Hibbing High School is rumored to be haunted by many ghosts, including:

The Ghost in Seat J-47: The most famous ghost at Hibbing High School is the ghost in seat J-47 of the auditorium. The ghost is said to be the spirit of a stage manager who died in the auditorium in 1942. Some people believe that the ghost is harmless, while others believe that it is mischievous and has even caused people to faint.

The Girl in the Dressing Room: Another popular ghost story at Hibbing High School is the story of the girl in the dressing room. The ghost is said to be the spirit of a young woman who died in a dressing room in the auditorium in the 1930s. Some people have claimed to see the ghost's reflection in the mirrors, while others have heard her crying.

The Man in the Basement: The man in the basement is another ghost that is rumored to haunt Hibbing High School. The ghost is said to be the spirit of a worker who was killed in the school's basement in the 1920s. Some people have claimed to see the ghost's shadow moving around in the basement, while others have heard his footsteps.

Ohio University

Ohio University in Athens, Ohio was founded in and has a rich history that spans over 200 years. There have been quite a few ghost stories that come from the buildings and houses associated with the university. Stories include former slaves associated with the Underground Railroad, an old insane asylum renovated by the University, former students who have died on campus, and an old lady who seems to not have left her.

Among Ohio University's haunted history, include:

The Ridges: The Ridges is a former psychiatric hospital that is now used as a museum and event space. It is rumored to be haunted by the ghosts of former patients, including a woman named Margaret Schilling who went missing from the hospital in 1978 and was later found dead. Visitors to the Ridges have reported seeing apparitions, hearing strange noises, and feeling cold spots.

Brown House: Brown House is a former dormitory that is now used as office space. It is rumored to be haunted by the ghosts of former students, including a group of children who drowned in the swimming pool that used to be located on the property. Visitors to Brown House have reported hearing children's voices and splashes coming from the pool area, even though the pool is no longer there.

Jefferson Hall: Jefferson Hall is a dormitory that is rumored to be haunted by the ghost of a former student named John. John is said to have died in the dormitory in the early 1900s, and his ghost is said to be responsible for many strange occurrences, including doors opening and closing by themselves, lights turning on and off by themselves, and objects moving around inexplicably.

Visitors have reported seeing apparitions in classrooms, libraries, and other buildings on campus.

Athens State College

Originally built in 1822 as the Athens Female Academy, then repurposed by the Methodist Church, later became the Athens State College. Local legend states that during the American Civil War, the structure was about to be burned to the ground by the invading Union army when the stern headmistress Jane Hamilton Childs presented the commanding officer a note from Abraham Lincoln himself. After reading it, the officer led his troops away.

Athens State University is rumored to be haunted by many ghosts, including:

The Ghost in the Elevator: The ghost in the elevator is said to be the spirit of a student who was killed in an elevator accident in the 1970s. The ghost is said to be seen in the elevator at night, and sometimes it will get stuck between floors.

The Ghost in the Library: The ghost in the library is said to be the spirit of a librarian who died in the library in the 1960s. The ghost is said to be seen walking through the library stacks at night, and sometimes it will move books around.

The Ghost in the Auditorium: The ghost in the auditorium is said to be the spirit of a student who died in the auditorium in the 1950s. The ghost is said to be seen sitting in the front row of the auditorium at night, and sometimes it will play the piano.

In addition to these specific ghosts, there have also been numerous reports of strange activity at the university, including lights turning on and off by themselves, doors opening and closing by themselves, footsteps and voices being heard in empty rooms, cold spots and apparitions being seen, and strange odors.

Stetson University

One of the structures that stand out at Stetson University is the 116-foot brick bell tower built in 1934. The tower was a gift from then professor of mathematics and engineering and later President of the University, Dr. Lincoln Hulley, and his family. The bell tower was designed and the construction was overseen by Dr. Hulley himself yet the very year the bell tower was complete, Dr.

Hulley died. Dr. Hulley intended for the bell tower to serve several purposes and for that, he succeeded.

At the top of the bell tower is the carillon appropriately named the Eloise Chimes after Dr. Hulley's wife. At the bottom, there is a huge room that is used on special occasions by the University but is also used to hold the body of Dr. Hulley and his wife Eloise who died around 25 years after her husband. Now named the Hulley Tower in honor of the professor it not only contains the eleven-bell chime set but also his crypt.

There have been numerous reports from students and some professors that have seen two apparitions walking around the tower and the grounds arm in arm. It seems the apparition of Dr. Hulley and his wife has been seen all over Stetson University and the surrounding neighborhood.

Stetson University is rumored to be haunted by several ghosts, including:

Elizabeth Stetson: Elizabeth Stetson was the third wife of Stetson University founder John B. Stetson. She is said to haunt Elizabeth Hall, a music building on campus. Some people have reported seeing her ghost walking the halls or playing the organ in the chapel.

P.D. Edmunds: P.D. Edmunds was the grounds secretary at Stetson University in the 1930s. He was murdered in Chaudoin Hall, an all-girls dormitory at the time. His ghost is said to haunt the building, and some people have reported hearing his footsteps or seeing his shadow.

The Ghost in the Clock Tower: The clock tower on campus is rumored to be haunted by the ghost of a student who fell to her death from the tower in the early 1900s. Some people have reported seeing her ghost standing at the top of the tower or ringing the bell.

Bowling Green State University

Bowling Green State University is a century-old college in the bustling of Bowling Green, in northeastern Ohio. First established in 1910, it is home to more than 20,000 students, over 200 undergraduate courses, and multiple known ghost hauntings.

It seems most universities carry legend of one ghost or another, but Bowling Green State University has a long history of hauntings by several ghosts, including:

Alice: Alice is said to be the ghost of an actress who died in the university's Eva Marie Saint Theatre in the early 1920s. She is often seen wearing a long white dress and has long, dark hair. Some people have reported seeing her walking the halls of the theatre or sitting in the audience during performances.

Amanda: Amanda is said to be the ghost of a Chi Omega sorority sister who died in a tragic accident during her initiation in the 1970s. She is often seen wandering the halls of the sorority house or sitting on a bench outside. Some people have reported hearing her crying or laughing at night.

The Ghost in the Library: The ghost in the library is said to be the spirit of a student who died in the university's library in the 1950s. He is often seen walking through the stacks or sitting at a table reading. Some people have reported hearing him whispering or seeing his shadow move out of the corner of their eyes.

In addition to these specific ghosts, there have also been numerous reports of strange activity at BGSU, including lights turning on and off by themselves, doors opening and closing by themselves, footsteps and voices being heard in empty rooms, cold spots, and apparitions being seen and strange odors.

CHAPTER ELEVEN
HAUNTED PRISONS

There's no denying that people experience some of the darkest points in their lives within prison walls. Locked securely behind walls and bars, the guilty have pondered their mistakes. Some have learned their lessons, and, once released, never looked back. But for some souls, their sentences have continued, even after death

The amount of pain, trauma, and terror associated with these facilities makes them inevitable hotspots for supernatural activity.

The Ghosts Of Alcatraz

Located in the San Francisco Bay, Alcatraz Island in San Francisco Bay, California is one of the most infamous prisons in the world, and it is also rumored to be one of the most haunted places in the United States.

Alcatraz was a federal prison from 1934 to 1963, and it housed some of the most notorious criminals of the era, including Al Capone, Machine Gun Kelly, and the Birdman of Alcatraz. The prison was known for its harsh conditions and its reputation as an escape-proof island.

The Native Americans mentioned the evil spirits they purportedly encountered on the island long before it became a federal prison. Mark Twain documented the eerie atmosphere of the island after visiting it, and described it as "being as cold as winter, even in the summer months."

Prisoners, rangers, and visitors have reported a wide range of alleged ghostly activity on Alcatraz, from whispering in cells and locked cell doors shutting, to phantom figures in corridors, cold spots, and even the sounds of musical instruments and sewing machines. Officials for Alcatraz have dismissed the reports of ghosts at Alcatraz as nonsense and deny their existence.

Since the prison closed, Alcatraz has become a popular tourist destination, and it is also a hot spot for paranormal investigators. There have been numerous reports of strange activity on the island, including footsteps and voices being heard in empty rooms, doors opening and closing by themselves, lights turning on and off by themselves, apparitions being seen, cold spots being felt and strange odors being smelled.

Some people believe that the ghosts of the former inmates still haunt the island, while others believe that the ghosts of the prison guards or other individuals who lived or worked on the island remain.

One of the most famous ghost stories at Alcatraz is the story of the "Cell 14-D Ghost." Cell 14-D was a solitary confinement cell that was known for its harsh conditions. It is said that several inmates died in Cell 14-D, and their ghosts are said to haunt the cell.

Another popular ghost story at Alcatraz is the story of the "Birdman." Robert Stroud, also known as the "Birdman of Alcatraz", was a prisoner at Alcatraz from 1942 to 1959. He was known for his love of birds, and he was allowed to keep several birds in his cell. Stroud died in 1963, but his ghost is said to be seen wandering the island with his birds.

While there is no scientific evidence to support the claims of hauntings at Alcatraz, the stories continue to circulate. Many people believe that the island's dark history and its isolation from the mainland make it a prime location for paranormal activity.

Haunted Yuma Territorial Prison

The Yuma Territorial Prison in Yuma was a federal prison from 1876 to 1909, and it housed some of the most notorious criminals of the era, including murderers, robbers, and outlaws. The prison was known for its harsh conditions and its high mortality rate. Yuma held more than 3,000 criminals during its 33 years in operation from 1876 to 1909, more than 100 of whom died on the premises.

Tour Guides have reported feeling a chill near cell #14, where a prisoner named John Ryan committed suicide. Another unsettling spot is known as the "Dark Cell," where disruptive inmates were held in isolation.

Since the prison closed, there have been numerous reports of strange activity, including footsteps and voices being heard in empty cells, lights turning on and off by themselves, doors opening and closing by themselves, apparitions being seen, including the ghosts of inmates and guards, cold spots being felt, and strange odors being smelled.

Some people believe that the ghosts of the former inmates still haunt the prison, seeking justice or revenge. Others believe that the ghosts of the prison guards or other individuals who lived or worked in the prison remain.

One of the most famous ghost stories at the Yuma Territorial Prison is the story of the "Ghost of the Hanging Tree." The Hanging Tree was located in the prison yard, and it was where many inmates were executed. It is said that the ghost of a young man who was hanged from the tree still haunts the area.

Another popular ghost story at the prison is the story of the "Ghost of the Dark Cell." The Dark Cell was a solitary confinement cell that was known for its harsh conditions. It is said that the ghost of a woman who was imprisoned in the Dark Cell still haunts the cell.

The Yuma Territorial Prison is now a state historic park, and it is open to the public for tours.

Eastern State Penitentiary

Eastern State Penitentiary in Philadelphia, Pennsylvania is widely considered to be one of the most haunted prisons in the United States. It was used from 1829 to 1971, and it housed some of the most notorious criminals of the era, including Al Capone and Willie Sutton. The prison was known for its solitary confinement system, which was designed to rehabilitate prisoners through reflection and remorse.

During its 142 years of service as an active prison, 1,200 inmates died. More than 50 inmates committed suicide, and over a dozen were murdered by other inmates. With all that trauma, there is no wonder why the spirits still roam the grounds.

From the 1940s, inmates and officers reported "mysterious visions and eerie experiences." Since it was abandoned, ghost sightings have increased tenfold. Paranormal researchers flock there to find signs of abnormal activity.

Notorious gangster Al Capone, who served time there, is said to have been "transformed into a weeping and terrified mess who would send out bloodcurdling screams at night, shouting for 'Jimmy' to 'leave me alone.'"

One of the most famous ghost stories at Eastern State Penitentiary is the story of the "Cell Block 12 Ghost." It was the most isolated in the prison, and it was where the most dangerous inmates were housed. It is said that the ghost of an inmate who was tortured in Cell Block 12 still haunts there.

Eastern State Penitentiary is now a museum, and it is open to the public for tours.

Old Idaho Penitentiary

Known as the first prison built in the state of Idaho; the penitentiary located east of Boise had housed over 13,000 inmates which also included 215 women. Like with most prisons, several inmates have died over the years which can lead to several unexplained and possibly paranormal
events.

The Penitentiary housed some of the most ruthless criminals such as Raymond Snowden, who was known as the Idaho Jack Ripper. He brutally murdered a woman and was sentenced to die by hanging. Stories have it that he hung for 15 minutes on the gallows inside of the prison in 1957. It is said he haunts the former prison and a cigar store in downtown Boise called Hanafin's.

People have reported strange noises, rattling of the walls, wails, and apparitions throughout the years. Visitors have also stated that they have been touched or pushed by someone within the prison walls. Some people have had the feeling of being watched. Others have reported seeing figures tending to the beautiful rose gardens within the prison property.

Some ghosts never leave the place of their death while some can move on to the other side. At the Old Idaho Penitentiary, some things were meant to stay behind those walls forever.

The Old Idaho Penitentiary is rumored to be haunted by several ghosts, including:

The Ghost of Cell 5 Block: This ghost is said to be the spirit of a man who was hanged in Cell 5 Block in the early 1900s. He is often seen standing in the cell, and some people have claimed to hear his footsteps or hear him talking.

The Ghost of the Infirmary: The ghost of the infirmary is said to be the spirit of a woman who died in the infirmary in the 1940s. She is often seen walking the halls of the infirmary, and some people have claimed to see her sitting in a rocking chair.

The Ghost of the Chapel: The ghost of the chapel is said to be the spirit of a priest who died in the chapel in the 1960s. He is often seen walking the aisles of the chapel, and some people have claimed to hear him singing hymns.

Waverly Hills Sanatorium

Waverly Hills Sanatorium in Louisville, Kentucky has a reputation for being haunted. It was a tuberculosis sanatorium from 1910 to 1961, and it is estimated that over 60,000 people died there. The sanatorium was known for its harsh conditions and its high mortality rate.

The sanatorium started as a one-room schoolhouse in the late 1800s. The Board of Tuberculosis Hospital later purchased the land and built the sanatorium, which opened in 1910 as a small quarantine for patients. The large building that now sits abandoned was built in 1926 in response to the need for a larger facility; the sanatorium could house over 400 patients.

Waverly Hills was closed in 1961 after an antibiotic that cured tuberculosis was discovered. However, it's believed that some patients never left and still haunt the grounds.

One of the most famous haunted places at the sanatorium is the "Body Chute." It was a tunnel that was used to transport the bodies of deceased patients to the morgue. It is said that the ghosts of patients who were sent into the chute still haunt the tunnel.

Another popular ghost story at the sanatorium is the story of the "Ghost of Room 502." This room in the sanatorium was used to house patients with mental illnesses. It is said that the ghost of a patient who died in Room 502 still haunts the room.

Waverly Hills Sanatorium is now a museum, and it is open to the public for tours.

Rise Of The Snow Queen Book Four Releasing January 2024

About the Author

G.W. Mullins

Thanks for choosing this book, if you enjoyed it, please leave positive feedback.

G.W. Mullins is an Author, Photographer, and Entrepreneur of Native American / Cherokee descent. He has been a published author for over 14 years. His writing has focused on the paranormal and Native American studies.

Mullins has released several books on the history/stories/fables of the Native American Indians. Among his books are the extremely successful "Star People, Sky Gods and Other Tales of the Native American Indians," "Story Teller An Anthology Of Folklore From The Native American Indians," "The Native American Story Book - Stories Of The American Indians For Children Volumes 1-5," "The Native American Cookbook," and "Walking With Spirits Native American Myths, Legends, And Folklore Volumes 1 Thru 6."

He has released the complete series of his Sci/fi Fantasy books "From The Dead Of Night," including the Best-Selling titles – "Daniel Is Waiting" and "Daniel Returns." His most recent work includes the series "Rise Of The Snow Queen" featuring Book One "The Polar Bear King",

Book Two "War Of The Witches", and Book Three "The Story of Gerda And Kai."

Mullins' latest releases include two young adult fantasy series, "Rise of the Darklighter" Book One "Dark Awakening," Book Two "Night Of The Demon" and the "Dream Walker" Book Series featuring "Enter the Sandman" and "Wide Awake In Dream Land." Among his other releases are "The Legend Of White Bear (Extended edition)" a Native American paranormal shapeshifting story, "Messages from The Other Side" (a nonfiction book about communication with the dead), and the currently releasing "The Convergence" (a post-apocalyptic book multi-series event).

For further information, on his writing, visit G.W. Mullins' website at ***http://gwmullins.wix.com/books***.

<u>Also Available From G.W. Mullins</u>

The Convergence Book Zero Mass Destruction

The Convergence Book One Armageddon

Rise of the Darklighter Book One Dark Awakening

Rise of the Darklighter Book Two Night Of The Demon

Rise Of The Snow Queen Book Three The Story Of Gerda And Kai

Rise Of The Snow Queen Book Two The War Of The Witches

Rise Of The Snow Queen Book One The Polar Bear King

Daniel Awakens A Ghost Story Begins– From The Dead Of Night Prequel

Daniel Is Waiting A Ghost Story – From The Dead Of Night Book One

Daniel Returns A Ghost Story - From The Dead Of Night Book Two

Daniel's Fate A Ghost Story Ends - From The Dead Of Night Book Four

Dream Walker Book Two Wide Awake In Dream Land

Dream Walker Book One Enter The Sand Man

Haunted America

Nick Grainger Book One The Curse Of Cleopatra

The Legend Of White Bear (Extended Edition)

Messages From The Other Side Stories of the Dead, Their Communication, and Unfinished Business

Vengeance – A Paranormal Mystery

Mysteries Of The Unseen World – Ghost, Hauntings and The Unexplained

Haunted America Stories Of Ghost, Hauntings And The Unexplained

Timeless – A Paranormal Romance Murder Mystery
Star People, Sky Gods, And Other Tales Of The Native American Indians

More Star People, Sky Gods, And Other Paranormal Tales Of The Native American Indians

Aliens, Gods, and other Paranormal Native American Tales

Buffalo Tales Of The Native American Indians

Coyote Tales Of The Native American Indians

Bear Tales Of The Native American Indians

Lost Tales Of The Native American Indians Vol 1

Lost Tales Of The Native American Indians Vol 2

Walking With Spirits Native American Myths, Legends,
And Folklore Volumes One Thru Six

The Native American Cookbook

Native American Cooking - An Indian Cookbook With
Legends And Folklore

The Native American Story Book - Stories Of The
American Indians For Children
Volumes One Thru Five

The Best Native American Stories For Children

Cherokee A Collection of American Indian Legends,
Stories And Fables

Creation Myths - Tales Of The Native American Indians
Strange Tales Of The Native American Indians

Spirit Quest - Stories Of The Native American Indians

Animal Tales Of The Native American Indians

Medicine Man - Shamanism, Natural Healing, Remedies
And Stories Of The Native American Indians

Native American Legends: Stories Of The Hopi Indians
Volumes One and Two

Totem Animals Of The Native Americans

Haunted America

The Best Native American Myths, Legends And Folklore
Volumes One Thru Three

Ghosts, Spirits And The Afterlife In Native American
Indian Mythology And Folklore

War Song: Tales Of The Native American Indians

Origin Tales Of The Native American

For books available from G.W. Mullins in Hardback,
Paperback and eBook

Visit: https://gwmullins.wixsite.com/books

Or scan the QR Code below

Links to G.W. Mullins pages are on Linktree
https://linktr.ee/gw.mullins

www.ingramcontent.com/pod-product-compliance
Lightning Source LLC
Chambersburg PA
CBHW070912120626
46546CB00001B/233